Routledge Revivals

Three Essays on Taxation in Simple General Equilibrium Models

This book, first published in 1984, examines the use of simple general equilibrium models in analysing the effects of taxes. The replacement of the earlier partial equilibrium approach has yielded numerous insights and conclusions, and these are examined here alongside the simple general equilibrium reasoning.

Three Essays on Taxation in Simple General Equilibrium Models

Neil Bruce

Routledge
Taylor & Francis Group

First published in 1984
by Garland Publishing, Inc.

This edition first published in 2021 by Routledge
2 Park Square, Milton Park, Abingdon, Oxon, OX14 4RN
and by Routledge
605 Third Avenue, New York, NY 10017

Routledge is an imprint of the Taylor & Francis Group, an informa business

Publisher's Note
The publisher has gone to great lengths to ensure the quality of this reprint but points out that some imperfections in the original copies may be apparent.

Disclaimer
The publisher has made every effort to trace copyright holders and welcomes correspondence from those they have been unable to contact.

A Library of Congress record exists under LCCN: 79053822

ISBN 13: 978-0-367-76580-4 (hbk)
ISBN 13: 978-1-003-16762-4 (ebk)

DOI: 10.4324/9781003167624

Three Essays on Taxation in Simple General Equilibrium Models

Neil Bruce

Garland Publishing, Inc.
New York & London, 1984

Library of Congress Cataloging in Publication Data

Bruce, Neil.
Three essays on taxation in simple general equilibrium models.

(Outstanding dissertations in economics)
Thesis (Ph.D.)—University of Chicago, 1976.
Bibliography: p.
1. Taxation—Mathematical models. I. Title. II. Series.
HJ2305.B78 1984 336.2'00724 79-53822
ISBN 0-8240-4170-4

All volumes in this series are printed on acid-free, 250-year-life paper.

Printed in the United States of America

THE UNIVERSITY OF CHICAGO

THREE ESSAYS ON TAXATION IN SIMPLE GENERAL EQUILIBRIUM MODELS

A DISSERTATION SUBMITTED TO

THE FACULTY OF THE DIVISION OF THE SOCIAL SCIENCES

IN CANDIDACY FOR THE DEGREE OF

DOCTOR OF PHILOSOPHY

DEPARTMENT OF ECONOMICS

BY

NEIL BRUCE

CHICAGO, ILLINOIS

MARCH 1976

TABLE OF CONTENTS

APPENDICES

ACKNOWLEDGMENTS

During the writing of this dissertation, I was fortunate enough to receive suggestions, comments and constructive criticism from numerous persons. First of all, I would like to thank the members of my thesis committee: Arnold Harberger, William Brock and Larry Sjaastad for giving me the benefits of their knowledge and experience during the various stages of this thesis. I would also like to single out Frank Flatters, Jacob Frenkel, Harry Johnson and Don Richter among others who offered constructive suggestions on earlier drafts. Also, grateful acknowledgment is made of the financial support I received throughout my graduate studies at the University of Chicago from the Canada Council, the Ford and Lilly Foundations. I would also like to express my gratitude and devotion to another "financial supporter"--my wife Janis, who also gave me emotional and moral support throughout the writing of this thesis. Finally, I would like to thank Alyce Monroe for typing the manuscript.

LIST OF ILLUSTRATIONS

INTRODUCTION

The use of simple general equilibrium models for analyzing the effects of taxes has virtually replaced the earlier partial equilibrium approach and has, in the process, yielded numerous insights and conclusions. The reason for this change is the recognition that the failure to include indirect effects in and interactions with markets not directly affected by a tax is a serious omission, especially for major taxes such as the corporation income tax, trade taxes and excise taxes involving a substantial industry in the economy. It is this context of simple general equilibrium reasoning which provides the unifying theme relating the three separate taxation topics which constitute this dissertation.

The subject of tax incidence has been considerably advanced by the application of general equilibrium theory. But while the general equilibrium work is recognized as a marked improvement over the naive forward and backward shifting concepts of partial analysis, some of its conclusions have been questioned on the grounds that they are obtained by extrapolating elasticity values determined by differential analysis around the initial or terminal equilibrium. This is deemed inappropriate for large, discrete tax changes. Also, the assumption of identical and homothetic tastes, which general equilibrium models usually include, are criticized on the grounds that such an assumption precludes any incidence effects operating through changes in relative commodity prices as well as changes in factor prices. In Chapter I, these two issues are addressed directly. It is demonstrated

 DOI: 10.4324/9781003167624-1

that the inclusion of second order terms does not significantly change the linear approximations. In addition, a simple model involving differing tastes among factor owners is constructed and an analysis of total incidence based on both changes in relative commodity and factor prices is presented.

In Chapter II, the use of consumer's surplus welfare cost indexes for measuring the potential welfare losses resulting from tax induced distortions in commodity markets is examined. The main issue is found not to be whether general equilibrium considerations are ignored in the construction of such indexes (in general, they are not) but that the value of the consumer's surplus index for a specific vector of taxes is not invariant to the order in which the tax elements are imposed or changed. This occurs because the general equilibrium demand function, under which the consumer's surplus areas are calculated, does not necessarily satisfy the integrability conditions. In this chapter, this problem is shown to be of the nature of the general index number problem and that the consumer's surplus index is a form of the Divisia quantity index. It is then demonstrated that in principle it is possible to normalize nominal prices so as to make this Divisia index invariant to the order of the taxes and that under these circumstances, this index will accurately indicate whether welfare has risen or fallen. Three normalizations are given corresponding to the cases of homothetic preferences, "parallel" indifference surfaces and the utility function underlying linear expenditure systems.

The prevalent assumption that the total capital stock is fixed is relaxed in Chapter III so as to examine the effects of the opening of trade and of variations in trade taxes on long-run steady state values in an economy which is inter-temporally maximizing. For example, the optimal steady state capital stock is found to increase or decrease upon the opening of trade depending on whether the country has a comparative advantage in the capital or labor intensive commodity. The effects of trade taxes on the steady state capital stock and level of consumption are found by differentiating the steady state conditions. Finally, the case of a small country facing fixed terms of trade is considered and most of the results derived for a moderate size economy are found to hold in this case except that the country will generally specialize when facing fixed terms of trade.

CHAPTER I

SOME EXTENSIONS OF THE TWO SECTOR GENERAL EQUILIBRIUM MODEL OF TAX INCIDENCE

The analysis of tax incidence is concerned with the redistributive effects of taxation among individuals or groups of individuals in society. The identity of these groups is determined by the nature of the tax and the interests of the researcher, but generally individuals are grouped according to factor ownership, level of income, commodity preference or other such distinction. While the term incidence is often used to refer to the "primary" burden of the tax, this can lead to the erroneous conclusion that the effect of a tax on a particular group's income lies between 0 and 100 percent of the tax proceeds. In fact, the total distributive consequences of a tax depend on how the tax affects relative prices, particularly factor returns, and the distributive effect on a given group can exceed 100 percent or be less than 0 percent of the tax proceeds, the latter being a case where the group gains as a result of the tax.[1]

As a result, modern incidence analysis is concerned with the effect of taxes on relative prices and it is assumed that the tax proceeds are redistributed or spent in a way that is neutral with respect to the relevant

---

[1]A. C. Harberger deals at some length with the "no-gain fallacy" in "Corporation Income Taxes," in International Encyclopedia of the Social Sciences (New York: Crowell Collier, 1968), Vol. 15, Part III, pp. 538-45 which is reprinted in Arnold C. Harberger, Taxation and Welfare (Boston: Little, Brown and Co., 1974), pp. 122-33.

DOI: 10.4324/9781003167624-2

groups. This approach necessarily involves the general equilibrium determination of relative prices, and the two good, two factor model used extensively by trade theorists has proven useful for this purpose.

The starting point is the well known analysis of differential tax incidence[1] in an economy consisting of consumers possessing identical, homothetic utility functions. In this case, the effect of a tax on relative commodity prices can be ignored so the analysis concentrates on the effect of a tax on relative factor prices. As it stands, the analysis of Harberger and Mieszkowski gives the (logarithmic) differential change in the factor price ratio resulting from a differential change in a sales or partial factor tax. In the first part of this chapter this analysis is extended to the case of discrete tax increments using first and second order approximations. In the second part of the chapter, I return to differential analysis but relax the assumption of identical preferences among the consumers.

The Two Sector Model of Tax Incidence

There are two goods X_1 and X_2 produced according to linear homogeneous production functions using two factors, labor (L) and homogeneous capital (K), for which the stocks are fixed in the total economy. It is assumed that the corporation income tax can be represented by a partial factor tax t_c denoting the *ad valorem* tax rate on the earnings of capital used in producing X_1 which can be viewed as the composite corporate good. In addition, the incidence of a sales tax on X_1 is analyzed with t_s denoting the *ad valorem* sales tax rate on X_1. The production side of this

[1]Arnold C. Harberger, "The Incidence of the Corporation Income Tax," *Journal of Political Economy* 70 (June 1962):215-40 and Peter Mieszkowski, "On the Theory of Tax Incidence," *Journal of Political Economy* 75 (June 1967):250-62.

simple economy is represented by equations (1.1) to (1.4) below:[1]

(1.1) $$a_{L1}X_1 + a_{L2}X_2 = L$$

(1.2) $$a_{K1}X_1 + a_{K2}X_2 = K$$

(1.3) $$a_{L1}p_L + a_{K1}p_K T_c = pT_s$$

(1.4) $$a_{L2}p_L + a_{K2}p_K = 1\,.$$

In the above equations, a_{ij} is the number of units of factor i used producing a unit of X_j, p_L and p_K are the net factor prices of labor and capital services respectively, p is the gross of tax relative price of X_1 (X_2 is the numeraire good) and T_c and T_s equal $1/1-t_c$ and $1-t_s$ respectively. Therefore, $p_K T_c$ is the gross of tax price of capital's services and pT_s is the net of tax price received by the firms producing X_1.[2]

Taking the total logarithmic derivatives of equations (1.1) through (1.4) we obtain the general equilibrium supply curve (in differential form) as equation (1.5) and the Stolper-Samuelson relationship as equation (1.8) below. The details of the derivation follow Jones and are reproduced in Appendix A. Then,

(1.5) $$DX_1 - DX_2 = \frac{\delta_1\sigma_1 + \delta_2\sigma_2}{|v|\,|z|}(Dp + DT_s) - \frac{v_{K2}\delta_1\sigma_1 + v_{K1}\delta_2\sigma_2}{|v|\,|z|}DT_c$$

where D denotes the logarithmic differential operator, $z_{Lj} = L_j/L$ is the

---

[1]The reader will recognize the following as the formulation of the two sector model developed by Ronald Jones where his λ_{ij}, θ_{ij} are my z_{ij}, v_{ij} respectively. See Ronald W. Jones, "The Structure of Simple General Equilibrium Models," Journal of Political Economy 73 (December 1965):557-72.

[2]While this notation is convenient, it should be noted that an increase in t_s is represented by $DT_s < 0$.

physical share of labor in producing X_j, $z_{Kj} = K_j/K$ is the physical share of capital in sector j, $v_{ij} = p_i a_{ij}/p_j X_j$ is the value share of factor i in producing good X_j, σ_j is the elasticity of substitution of factors in sector j, $\delta_j = z_{Lj}v_{Kj} + z_{Kj}v_{Lj} > 0$, and $DT_s = -Dt_s$ $(t_s \neq 0)$ while $DT_c = Dt_c/1-t_c$ $(0 < t_c < 1)$. In addition:

$$(1.6) \qquad |z| = (z_{L1}-z_{K1}) = (z_{K2}-z_{L2}) = \frac{X_1X_2}{LK}(a_{L1}a_{K2}-a_{K1}a_{L2}) \neq 0$$

$$(1.7) \qquad |v| = (v_{L1}-v_{L2}) = (v_{K2}-v_{K1}) = \frac{p_Lp_K}{pT_s}\left(\frac{a_{L1}a_{K2}}{T_c} - a_{K1}a_{L2}\right) \neq 0.$$

From equations (1.6) and (1.7) it is clear that the sign of $|z|$ and $|v|$ depend on the physical and value factor intensities of the sectors respectively, and that when $T_c = 1$ $(t_c = 0)$ their signs will be the same.

The Stolper-Samuelson relationship between relative commodity prices and relative factor prices is expressed as:

$$(1.8) \qquad Dp_K-Dp_L = \frac{-(Dp + DT_s - v_{K1}DT_c)}{|v|}.$$

Since consumers' tastes are identical and homothetic, the demand side of the model can be expressed by:

$$(1.9) \qquad DX_1 - DX_2 = -\sigma_D\,Dp$$

where σ_D is the elasticity of substitution in consumption. Solving (1.5), (1.7) and (1.9) to get:

$$(1.10) \qquad Dp_K-Dp_L = \frac{(v_{K1}\sigma_D|z| - \delta_1\sigma_1)DT_c - (\sigma_D|z|)DT_s}{\delta_1\sigma_1 + \delta_2\sigma_2 + |z||v|\sigma_D}$$

which is the percentage change in the rental-wage ratio resulting from differential increments in the taxes. Setting $DT_s = 0$ expression (1.10) gives the percentage change in the factor price ratio resulting from a very small increment in the partial factor tax on capital in producing X_1. Since $|z|$ and $|v|$ have the same sign when $T_c = 1$ and the δ_i and σ_i are positive, the denominator is always positive providing the initial equilibrium was one where $t_c = 0$ or is very small. Therefore the effect of the tax on p_K/p_L depends solely on the sign of the numerator which is necessarily negative if $|z| < 0$ which obtains when X_1 is capital intensive. Thus we have Harberger's conclusion that a tax on capital in the capital intensive industry must lower the relative return to capital. On the other hand, if $|z|$ is sufficiently large and positive (and particularly if $v_{K1}\sigma_D$ is large while $\delta_1\sigma_1$ is small) the numerator can be positive, and a tax on capital imposed only in the labor intensive industry may raise the relative return to capital.[1]

If $DT_c = 0$, expression (1.10) gives minus the percentage change in the rental-wage ratio resulting from a differential increment in the sales tax on X_1. In this case, the effect on the factor price ratio depends on the sign of $|z|$ and for a positive increment in the sales tax (i.e., $-DT_s > 0$) will cause:

$$Dp_K - Dp_L \gtrless 0 \quad \text{as} \quad |z| \gtrless 0.$$

That is, the rental-wage ratio will rise or fall as a result of a differential increase in the sales tax on X_1 depending on whether X_1 is capital or labor intensive. Finally it should be noted that as $\sigma_1 \to 0$, the partial factor tax on capital becomes equivalent to a sales tax on X_1 of $-DT_s/v_{K1}$.

The above expression was derived for infinitesimal changes in taxes. In extending these results to discrete tax increments, consideration must be

---

[1] Harberger, "The Incidence of the Corporation Income Tax," pp. 227-30.

given to the possibility that the coefficients in expression (1.10) can change as the tax increases thereby changing the expression itself. For example, Jones[1] has demonstrated that sufficiently large values of partial factor taxes can cause the signs of $|v|$ and/or $|z|$ to change, that is the value and/or physical factor intensities of the goods can be reversed. Under these circumstances, the usual qualitative conclusions of incidence analysis reviewed above may not be valid. Moreover, the case of partial factor taxes, the direction of the effect of such a tax on the factor price ratio may be reversed even if there are no factor intensity reversals.

Discrete Changes in Partial Factor Taxes

The following analysis will concentrate on the corporation income tax analysis of Harberger. Setting $DT_s = 0$, expression (1.10) becomes:

$$(1.11) \qquad Dp_K - Dp_L = \left[\frac{v_{K1}\sigma_D|z| - \delta_1\sigma_1}{\delta_1\sigma_1 + \delta_2\sigma_2 + \sigma_D|z||v|}\right] DT_c$$

where the expression in the square brackets is an elasticity coefficient between the factor price ratio p_K/p_L and T_c and will be referred to as E_{fT}. This expression differs from Harberger's expression (12) only in notation, the choice of the numeraire, and the specification of the demand parameter as the elasticity of substitution rather than the elasticity of demand. Inserting the following post-tax parameter values used by Harberger[2]

$$v_{K1} = 1/6 \qquad z_{L1} = 10/11 \qquad \sigma_1 = \sigma_D = 1$$

$$v_{K2} = 1/2 \qquad z_{K1} = 1/2 \qquad \sigma_2 = 1/2$$

---

[1] Ronald W. Jones, "Distortions in Factor Markets and the General Equilibrium Model of Production," Journal of Political Economy 79 (June 1971): 437-59.

[2] Harberger, "The Incidence of the Corporation Income Tax," pp. 227-32.

then E_{fT} can be evaluated as -.587 which is substituted into equation (1.11) to obtain:

(1.11') $$Dp_K - Dp_L = -.587\ DT_c\ .$$

The imposition of a 50 percent corporation income tax means that T_c increases from 1 to 2, and it is not clear a priori that this can be treated as a differential change. The corporation income tax has been imposed in an industry which is labor intensive in both physical and value terms according to the post-tax values of the parameters so unless both $|z|$ and $|v|$ have changed sign, we are not dealing with a case involving factor intensity reversals. Nevertheless, the sign of E_{fT} may have changed sign because the large value of T_c may have increased the physical labor intensity of the sector enough to cause $|z|$ to increase in value sufficiently to change the sign of the numerator in expression (1.11). Therefore, prior to the tax, the numerator could have been positive so that if we view the imposition of a discrete tax as a continuous process, the initial tax increments may have increased p_K/p_L, so using the post-tax value of -.587 may overstate the decline in the rental-wage ratio resulting from the imposition of the total tax. Before examining how E_{fT} varies with the value of T_c, it can be shown that even with constancy assumptions, the effect of a discrete tax can vary according to whether the slope or the elasticity is assumed constant.

Suppose it is assumed that the elasticity coefficient $E_{fT} = -.587$ is a constant and let the rental-wage ratio $p_K/p_L = \omega$. Equation (1.11') is written:

$$D\omega = -.587\ DT_c$$

which, letting the superscript 0 and 1 denote the pre- and post-tax values respectively, can be integrated from $T_c = 1$ to $T_c^1 = 2$ to obtain:

$$\ln \left(\frac{\omega^1}{\omega^0}\right) = -.587 \ln \left(\frac{T_C^1}{T_C^0}\right) = -.587 \ln 2.$$

or $\omega^1/\omega^0 = .67$. Since $\omega^1/\omega^0 = (p_K^1 K)(p_L^0 L)/(p_K^0 K)(p_L^0 L)$, the share received by capital fell by a third relative to labor as a result of the corporation income tax. Using Harberger's data it can further be concluded that capital's share of national income was .214 and .143 before and after the tax respectively.[1] Assuming total national income was unaffected by the tax, the change in capital's net earnings (ΔI_K) is calculated as $(p_K^1 - p_K^0)\cdot K = -.5\ p_K^1 K$ while the tax proceeds of a 50 percent corporation income tax will be equal to the net return to corporate capital that is, $R = p_K^1 K_1$. Therefore the ratio ΔI_K to R can be calculated to be

$$\frac{\Delta I_K}{R} = \frac{-.5\ p_K^1 K}{p_K^1 K_1} = \frac{-.5}{z_{K_1}} = -1.00\ .$$

---

[1]In Harberger, "The Incidence of the Corporation Income Tax," we find the net income to capital and labor in the post tax situation as

$$p_K^1 K = \$\ 40 \times 10^9$$

$$p_L^1 L = \$220 \times 10^9$$

while the tax proceeds equal $R = p_K^1 K_1 = \$20 \times 10^9$. Thus, $p_K^1 K = .143\ I^1$ where $I^1 = p_K^1 K + p_L^1 L + R$. Since

$$\frac{p_K^0 K}{p_L^0 L} = \frac{\omega^0}{\omega^1}\frac{p_K^1 K}{p_L^1 L} = \frac{.182}{.67} = .272$$

the earnings of capital prior to the imposition of the tax is calculated as $p_K^0 K = .214\ I^0$ where $I^0 = p_K^0 K + p_L^0 L$. Assuming total national income was inappreciably changed by the presence of the tax, $I^0 = I^1$ therefore $p_K^1 = .67\ p_K^0$ and $\Delta I_K = (p_K^1 - p_K^0)K = -.5\ p_K^1 K$.

This implies that the net income of capitalists as a whole fell by the amount of the tax proceeds.

Alternatively, it can be assumed that the slope coefficient $d\omega/dT_c$ is a constant. Since we observe the post-tax value

$$E_{fT} = \frac{d\omega}{dT_c} \cdot \frac{T_c^1}{\omega^1} = \frac{d\omega}{dT_c} \cdot \frac{2}{\omega^0 + d\omega/dT_c} = -.587$$

we can normalize $\omega^0 = 1$ and calculate $d\omega/dT_c = -.227$. Therefore:

$$\omega^1 = 1 + (d\omega/dT_c)(T_c^k - T_c^0) = .773.$$

In this case $\omega^1/\omega^0 = .773$ so the net share of capital has declined by less than 25 percent. The ratio between the change in the net income of capital and the tax proceeds is now calculated to be -.67.[1] The assumption that the slope term, rather than the elasticity coefficient, is constant yields the conclusion that the net income of capital fell by two-thirds of the tax revenues collected as compared to 100 percent in the previous case.

The difference between the assumption of a constant elasticity coefficient and a constant slope coefficient is illustrated in Figure 1. The curve EE represents the relationship between ω and T_c if the elasticity coefficient is a constant with ω^1/ω^0 as measured on the left vertical axis. The straight line SS (with slope of -.227) is the relationship if the slope term is assumed constant, where ω^1/ω^0 is now measured on the right vertical

---

[1]Since $\omega^1/\omega^0 = (p_K^1 K)(p_L^1 L)(p_K^0 K) = .773$ then $p_K^0 K/p_L^0 L = .2354$ and $p_K^0 K = .1906\ I^0$. Assuming $I^1 = I^0$ we find $p_K^1/p_K^0 = .75$. Therefore

$$\frac{\Delta I_K}{R} = \frac{-.333 p_K^1 K}{p_K^1 K_1} = \frac{-.333}{z_{K1}} = .67\ .$$

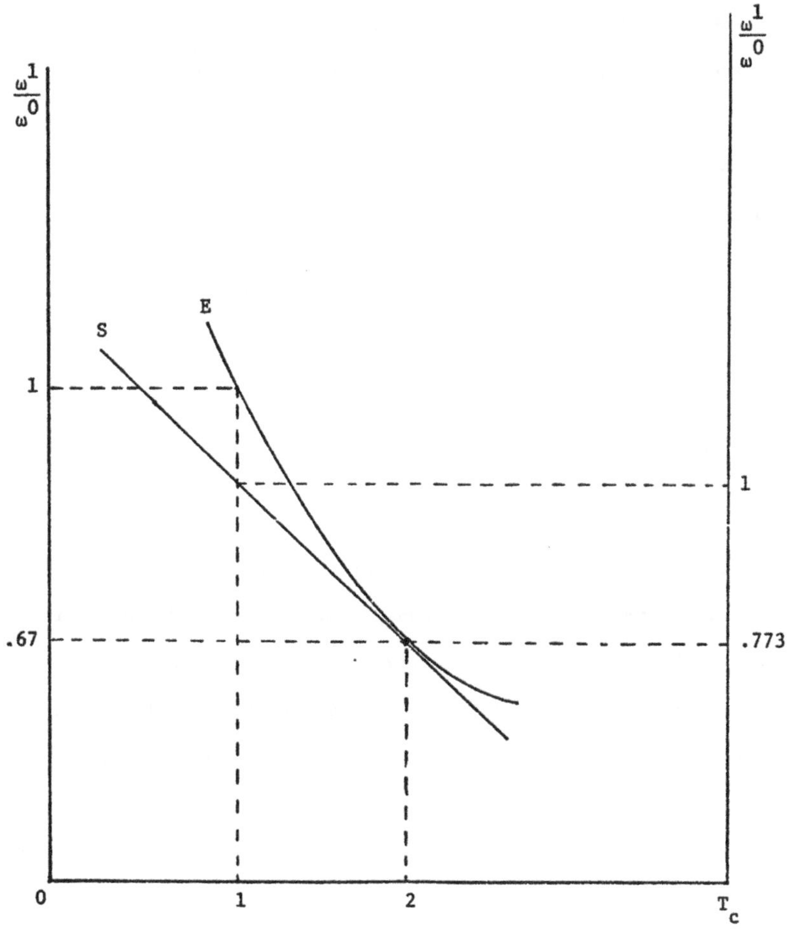

Fig. 1.--Graphical illustration of the difference between the constant slope and the constant elasticity assumptions.

axis. The two curves are tangent at point A on the basis of common post tax values.

The above two estimates of the incidence of the corporation income tax differed on the basis of which coefficient was assumed constant. Of course, the constancy of one implies the non-constancy of the other and vice versa. For example, if the slope term is assumed constant then it implies that:[1]

$$\frac{dE_{fT}}{E_{fT}} = DT_c - D\omega = (1-E_{fT})DT_c = 1.587\ DT_c$$

which, using the post-tax values of E^1_{fT} and T^1_c, implies:

$$\frac{dE_{fT}}{dT_c} = \frac{(1-E^1_{fT})\ E^1_{fT}}{T^1_c} = \frac{(1.587)(-.587)}{2} = -.46578\ .$$

In order to refine the accuracy of the incidence analysis when large discrete tax increments are being considered, a second order approximation is made by calculating how E_{fT} actually changes with T_c on the basis of known parameters. In Appendix A, the term E_{fT} in equation (1.11) is differentiated with respect to T_c assuming that all of the elasticities of substitution are constant. In this case we find that dE_{fT}/dT_c depends on the same parameters as E_{fT} itself, and using post tax values of the parameters we can calculate $dE_{fT}/dT_c \approx .1$. Therefore E_{fT} changes in the opposite direction to that implied by a constant slope term and the following second order approximations will increase the measured burden on capital as compared to approximations based on the constant slope assumption.

---

[1]This is obtained by differentiating $E_{fT} = (d\omega/dT_c)(T_c/\omega)$. Since E_{ft} is negative, $\ell n\ E_{fT}$ is not defined so the notation dE_{fT} is used.

Again two second-order constancy assumptions can be made; that the slope term dE_{fT}/dT_c is constant or that the elasticity $D|E_{fT}|/DT_c = (-dE_{fT}/dT_c)(T_c/|E_{fT}|)$ is a constant where $|E_{fT}|$ is the absolute value of E_{fT}.[1] When dE_{fT}/dT_c is assumed constant:

(1.12) $$E_{fT}(T_c) = E_{fT}(T_c^0) + .1\ (T_c-1).$$

By setting $T_c = T_c^1 = 2$ we can solve for $E_{fT}(T_c^0)$ and evaluate using post tax values as $E_{fT}^0 = -.687$. Substituting into equation (1.12) to get:

$$D\omega = (-.787 + .1\ T_c)\ DT_c$$

which is integrated to obtain:

$$\ell n\ (\omega^1/\omega^0) = -.787\ \ell n(T_c^1/T_c^0) + .1\ (T_c^1 - T_c^0) = -.446.$$

Therefore $\omega^1/\omega^0 = .641$ and $\Delta I_k/R = -1.093$.[2]

The elasticity coefficient can be calculated as:

$$\frac{D|E_{fT}|}{DT_c} = \frac{-\ 2\ (.1)}{.587} = -.3408$$

evaluated at post-tax values and assuming this elasticity is constant it can be integrated to obtain:

---

[1]Since E_{fT} doesn't change signs between T_c^0 and T_c^1, this transformation poses no problems.

[2]Since $\omega^1/\omega^0 = (p_K^1K)(p_L^0L)/(1_L^1L)(p_K^0K) = .641$, then $(p_K^0K)(p_L^0L) = .284$. Hence $p_K^0K = .22115\ I^0$ and assuming $I^1 = I^0$ we find $p_K^1/p_K^0 = .647$. Then $p_K^1 - p_K^0 = -.5465\ p_K^1$ and

$$\frac{\Delta I_k}{R} = \frac{-.5465p_K^1K}{p_K^1K_1} = \frac{-.5465}{z_{K1}} = -1.093.$$

$$(1.13)\qquad \ell n \left(\frac{|E^T_{fT}|}{|E^0_{fT}|} \right) = -.3408 \quad \ell n \left(\frac{T_c}{T^0_c} \right) = -.2362 \quad \text{when } T_c = 2.$$

Therefore $|E^1_{fT}|/|E^0_{fT}| = .79$ and $|E^0_{fT}| = .587/.79 = .743$. Substituting back into equation (1.13):

$$\ell n\ |E_{fT}| = \ell n\ |E^0_{fT}| - .3408\ \ell n\ T_c$$

so $|E_{fT}| = .743\ T_c^{-.3408}$. Equation (1.11) can now be written $D\omega = -|E^T_{fT}|DT_c$ and by substituting for $|E_{fT}|$ it can be integrated to obtain:

$$\ell n\ (\omega^1/\omega^0) = -.743 \int_{T^0_c}^{T^1_c} T_c^{-1.3408}\ dT_c$$

$$= \frac{.743}{.3408}\ (2^{-.3408} - 1) = -.4578.$$

Hence $\omega^1/\omega^0 = .6325$ and we can calculate the ratio of the change in capital's net earnings to tax proceeds is -1.125.[1] These results are summarized in Table 1 where the effects of a 50 percent corporation income tax on the factor price ratio and the net earnings of capital relative to the tax proceeds are listed for the first and second approximations considered above.

In summary, the calculation of second order terms tends to increase the burden of the corporate income tax on capital as compared to the constant elasticity and (especially) the constant slope assumptions. In fact, the second order approximations indicate capital's net earnings fall by

---

[1] $\omega^1/\omega^0 = (p^1_K K)(p^0_L L)/(1^1_L L)(p^0_K K) = .6325$ so $(p^0_K K)(p^0_L L) = .288$. Hence $p^0_K K = .223\ I^0$ and letting $I^0 = I^1$ to get $p^0_K/p^1_K = 1.5626$ and $p^1_K - p^0_K = -.5626\ p^1_K$. Therefore

$$\frac{\Delta I_k}{R} = \frac{-5626\ p^1_K K}{p^1_K K_1} = 1.125.$$

TABLE 1

THE INCIDENCE OF A 50 PERCENT CORPORATION INCOME TAX UNDER ALTERNATE ASSUMPTIONS

	Assumed Constant[a]	$\frac{\omega^1}{\omega^0} = \frac{p_K^1 K}{p_L^1 L} \frac{p_K^0 K}{p_L^0 L}$	$\frac{\Delta I_K}{R}$
First Order Approximations	$E_{fT} = \frac{d\omega}{dT_c} \frac{T_c}{\omega} = -.587$	.67	-1.00
	$\frac{d\omega}{dT_c} = -.227$	.773	- .67
Second Order Approximations	$\frac{dE_{fT}}{dT_c} = .1$	.641	-1.093
	$\frac{D\lvert E_{fT}\rvert}{DT_c} = -.3408$	.6325	-1.125

[a]All evaluated using post-tax values.

more than 100 percent of the taxes collected indicating that labor's earnings may be increased by the tax. The best first order approximation is obtained by assuming the elasticity term E_{fT} is constant.

Tax Incidence with Non-Identical Preferences

In the preceding analysis it was assumed that all consumers have identical, homothetic preferences in which case changes in relative commodity prices can be ignored for relative incidence purposes since all individuals are affected equally. In this case, the society was dichotomized into capitalists and laborers according to their (exclusive) factor ownership so that incidence depends only on changes in relative factor prices.

Now consider the case of s individuals classified into r groups such that within each group all individuals have identical homothetic preferences and have the same factor income shares, i.e., the proportion of income received from each factor is the same for every individual in the group. For each group g, the demand conditions can be expressed as:

(1.14a) $$DX_1^g = \eta_{11}^g\, Dp + DI^g$$

(1.14b) $$DX_2^g = -\eta_{22}^g\, Dp + DI^g$$

where the superscript g denotes the group aggregate and I^g is the net factor income of group g. The market demand conditions can be derived as:[1]

(1.15) $$DX_1 - DX_2 = -\bar{\sigma}_D\, Dp + \sum_g^r m^g DI^g$$

where $X_i = \sum_g^r X_i^g$, $DX_i = \sum_g^r (X_i^g/X_i)\, DX_i^g$ and $m^g = (X_1^g/X_1) - (X_2^g/X_2)$ which is positive or negative according to whether group g has a relative preference for good X_1 or X_2. The market elasticity of substitution in consumption is $\bar{\sigma}_D$ where:

$$\bar{\sigma}_D = \sum_g^r \left(\frac{X_1^g}{X_1}\eta_{11}^g + \frac{X_2^g}{X_2}\eta_{22}^g\right)$$

Furthermore,

(1.16) $$DI^g = \frac{p_L L^g}{I^g} Dp_L + \frac{p_K K^g}{I^g} Dp_K$$

$$= s_L^g(Dp_L - Dp_K) + Dp_K$$

---

[1]Note that if r = 1 so that g is the only group, then subtracting (1.14b) from (1.14a) gives equation (1.9) with $-\sigma_D = \eta_{11} + \eta_{22}$. Also, that $\Sigma_g^r\, m^g = 0$, therefore if m^g is equal for all g, then $m^g = 0$ and (1.15) reduces to (1.9).

where

$$s_L^g = \frac{p_L L^g}{I^g} = 1 - \frac{p_K K^g}{I^g} = 1 - s_K^g$$

and $p_L L^g + p_K K^g = I^g$ and L^g, K^g are assumed constant for each group. Substituting (1.16) into (1.15) we get:

$$(1.17) \qquad DX_1 - DX_2 = - \bar{\sigma}_D \, Dp + \sum_g^r m^g s_L^g \, (Dp_L - Dp_K)$$

since $\sum_g^r (X_1^g/X_1) - \sum_g^r (X_2^g/X_2) = \sum_g^r m^g = 0$. Solving simultaneously with production side equations (see Appendix A) to get:

$$(1.18) \qquad Dp_K - Dp_L = \frac{(\bar{\sigma}_D v_{K1}|z| - \delta_1\sigma_1)DT_c - \bar{\sigma}_D|z|DT_s}{\delta_1\sigma_1 + \delta_2\sigma_2 + |z|\,|v|\bar{\sigma}_D - |z|\cdot\sum_g s_L^g m^g} .$$

Expression (1.18) is identical to expression (1.10) except for the last term in the denominator which can be greater or less than zero. Since $\sum_g m^g = 0$, then if m^g is the same for all g it must be zero. In fact this is the case of identical homothetic preferences and equation (1.18) reduces to (1.10) exactly. Another interesting case arises when s_L^g is the same for each group g, so that the groups differ only in commodity preference. Since s_L^g can now be factored out, the last term in the denominator is zero in this case also and expression (1.18) again reduces to (1.10). But in this case, incidence analysis depends only on changes in relative commodity prices since relative factor price changes will affect all groups equally.

In general, the sign of $|z|\cdot\sum_g s_L^g m^g$ can be positive or negative. Since $\sum_g m^g = 0$, then providing all the m^g are not zero, i.e., tastes do differ among groups, some m^g will be positive and others negative corresponding to X_1 and X_2 preference respectively. All the s_L^g must lie between zero and unity with larger or smaller values of s_L^g corresponding to larger or smaller shares of income from labor respectively. In general, if groups with larger values of s_L^g prefer X_1, then $\sum_g s_L^g m^g > 0$ and the last term in the denominator will be positive or negative depending on whether X_1 is labor or capital intensive, that is whether $|z|$ is greater or less than zero. On the other hand, if groups with smaller values of s_L^g tend to prefer X_1 then $\sum_g s_L^g m^g < 0$ and the last term is negative or positive depending on whether X_1 is labor or capital intensive. Thus if groups tend to prefer the good intensive in the factor from which they receive more income <u>relative to the other groups</u>, the last term in the denominator will be positive so that its subtraction will tend to reduce the (positive) value of the denominator. Therefore the absolute effect on relative factor prices from a differential increment in one of the taxes will be greater or smaller depending on whether or not groups tend to prefer the good intensive in "their" factor, that is the factor which contributes a larger share of the groups income relative to other groups.

To clarify the foregoing, let there be only two groups, a and b. It is easily seen that in this case, $m^a = - m^b$ and the last term of the denominator equals $|z|\ m^a(s_L^a - s_L^b)$. If X_1 is labor intensive so that $|z| > 0$, the above term is positive or negative depending on whether m^a and $(s_L^a - s_L^b)$ have the same or different signs. They will have the same sign if group a prefers the good intensive in the factor which it receives a larger share of its income relative to group b--regardless of whether or not this factor contributes the nominally larger or smaller share of the group's income. When X_1 is capital intensive, the term is positive if m^a and $(s_L^a - s_L^b)$ have opposite signs which again will obtain when each group prefers the good intensive in "their" factor.

These results are intuitively evident from the reasoning accompanying

Figure 2 which is drawn, without loss of generality, on the assumption that X_1 is labor intensive. The pre-tax supply and demand curves S and D establish the pre-tax equilibrium at A with relative commodity price p_A and rental wage ratio $(p_K/p_L)_A$. Let S' represent the general equilibrium supply curve after a production tax on X_1 is imposed. If demand is independent of the tax, either because all groups have identical homothetic preferences or because every group receives the same proportion of its income from a factor, then D does not shift as a result of the tax so that the post-tax equilibrium is at B with lower net of tax relative commodity price p_B^n and higher rental-wage ratio $(p_K/p_L)_B$. When each group prefers the good intensive in "their" factor, the post-tax demand curve shifts to the left such as D' with equilibrium at C with net of tax relative commodity price p_C^n and rental-wage ratio $(p_K/p_L)_C$ which is greater than the value of $(p_K/p_L)_B$ established when the distribution effects are neutral. Conversely, if each group preferred the commodity intensive in the factor which contributes relatively less to that group's income, the tax on X_1 distributes income towards the group preferring X_1 thus shifting the demand curve to the right such as D". As a result, the new equilibrium at D involves a smaller rise in the rental-wage ratio (to $[p_K/p_L]_D$) than in the neutral case. It should be noted that D" cannot lie sufficiently to the right to cause the rental-wage ratio to fall as a result of the tax on the labor intensive good since this would yield a contradiction.[1]

Returning to equation (1.18) and recalling that it gives the effect of production and partial factor taxes on relative factor prices when tastes

---

[1]The demand curve shifted to the right because income was redistributed towards capitalists thus raising the income of groups who prefer X_1 relative to the other groups. But if D shifted too far to the right, the price of capital's services would fall.

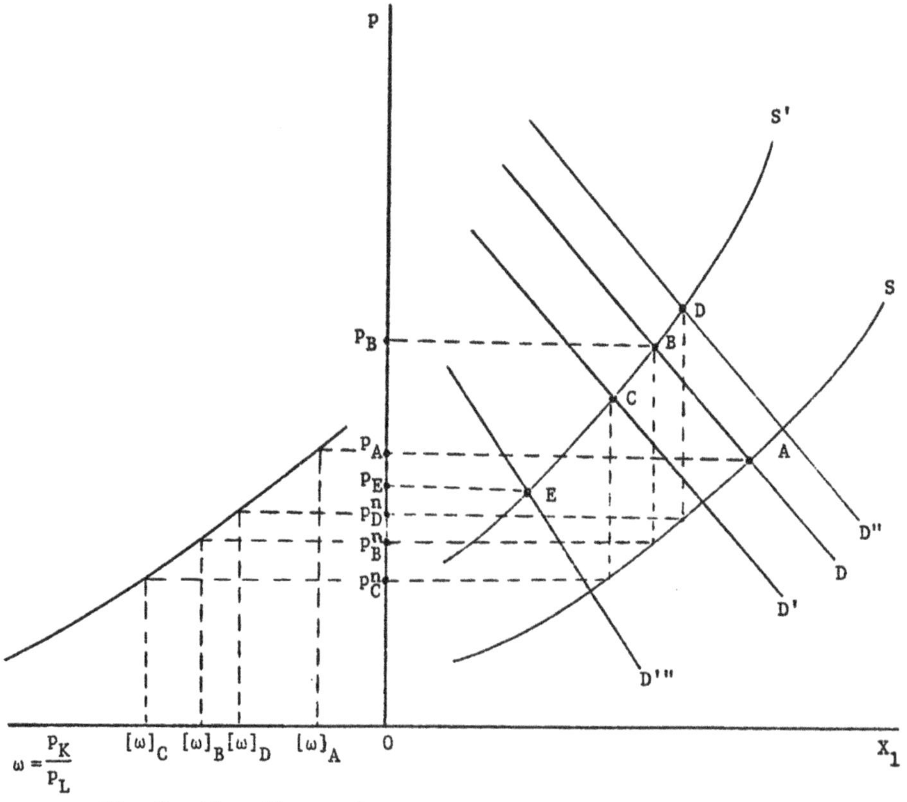

Fig. 2.--The effects of a sales tax on X_1 with alternative assumptions regarding the redistributive effect of the tax.

are not identical and factor shares differ, we can complete the analysis of tax incidence under these conditions by combining the effects of relative commodity price changes with that of relative factor price changes. Therefore the total incidence will involve both the effect of factor price changes, which has been the main focus of the general equilibrium approach, and the effect of relative commodity price changes with which the earlier partial equilibrium approaches to incidence were concerned. The total incidence will be calculated as the percentage change in the factor return received by a group minus the percentage change in the cost of purchasing the pre-tax bundle of commodities.[1] That is:

$$(1.19) \qquad Dy^g = [s_L^g \, Dp_L + (1 - s_L^g) \, Dp_K - s_1^g \, Dp]$$

where $s_1^g = pX_1^g/(pX_1^g + X_2^g)$ is the share of expenditure on good X_1 by group g, and y^g is the real income of group g. It is possible to solve (1.19) as a complicated expression involving DT_c now and DT_s, but instead suppose we want to consider how the taxes affect some group a relative to another group b. Using (1.19) we can write:

$$Dy^a - Dy^b = [(s_L^b - s_L^a)(Dp_K - Dp_L) + (s_1^b - s_1^a)Dp].$$

For simplicity, consider only a production or sales tax t_s where $T_s = 1-t_s$, then we can solve for $Dy^a - Dy^b$ in terms of DT_s using the production side equations (see Appendix A) to get:

$$(1.19) \qquad Dy^a - Dy^b = \frac{[(s_1^b - s_1^a)(|z| \Sigma\, m^g s_L^g - \delta_1\sigma_1 - \delta_2\sigma_2) - (s_L^b - s_L^a)\bar{\sigma}_D |z|] DT_s}{\delta_1\sigma_1 + \delta_2\sigma_2 + \bar{\sigma}_D |z| |v| - \Sigma\, m^g \, s_L^g \cdot |z|}$$

---

[1]Since only differential tax changes are being considered, problems involved using Laspeyres index do not arise.

If tastes are identical for all groups so that $s_1^b - s_1^a = \Sigma\, m^g s_L^g = 0$ but $s_L^b \neq s_L^a$, this expression simplifies to:

$$(1.19') \qquad Dy^a - Dy^b = \frac{-(s_L^b - s_L^a)\bar{\sigma}_D |z| DT_s}{\delta_1\sigma_1 + \delta_2\sigma_2 + \bar{\sigma}_D |z||v|}$$

and the differential incidence between two groups depends on the factor intensity of the taxed good and the difference in the share of labor between the two groups. Noting that $-DT_s > 0$ corresponds to an increase in the sales tax, then $Dy^a - Dy^b \gtrless 0$ as $(s_L^b - s_L^a)|z| \gtrless 0$. That is, the group which receives the smallest share of its income from the factor intensive in good X_1 will gain relative to the other group. If factor shares are identical for all groups while tastes are not so that $s_L^b - s_L^a = \Sigma\, m^g s_L^g = 0$ and $s_1^a \neq s_1^b$, then expression (1.19) reduces to:

$$(1.19'') \qquad Dy^a - Dy^b = \frac{-(s_1^b - s_1^a)(\delta_1\sigma_1 + \delta_2\sigma_2)}{\delta_1\sigma_1 + \delta_2\sigma_2 + \bar{\sigma}_D |z||v|} DT_s \, .$$

If we consider a tax increase (where $-DT_s > 0$), then $Dy^a - Dy^b \gtrless 0$ as $s_1^b \gtrless s_1^a$ hence the group with the lower (marginal and average) propensity to consume X_1 will gain relative to the other group.

When groups differ in both tastes and factor shares, the relative incidence is ambiguous without specifying parameter values. For simplicity let a and b be the only groups, then for an increase in the sales tax on X_1 (that is, $-DT_s > 0$) we have (see Appendix A for the details):

$$(1.20) \qquad Dy^a - Dy^b \gtrless 0 \quad \text{as}$$

$$[(s_1^b - s_1^a)(\delta_1\sigma_1 + \delta_2\sigma_2) + |z|(s_L^b - s_L^a)(\bar{\sigma}_D + m^a(s_1^b - s_1^a))] \gtrless 0$$

where $m^a(s_1^b - s_1^a) < 0$. As a result, the second expression in the square brackets is ambiguous in sign even though $|z|$ and $(s_L^b - s_L^a)$ may be specified as to sign. This leads to an interesting result which is not apparent from partial analysis. That is, on the basis of partial analysis (where either tastes or factor shares but not both differ), it might be concluded that a group which prefers the taxed good and receives a larger share of its income from the factor intensive in the taxed good must lose on both the factor and commodity price sides and hence must lose relative to the other group. But expression (1.20) demonstrates that this is not so. For example, let X_1 be labor intensive with group b preferring good X_1 and receiving the larger share of its income from labor. Even though $|z|$, $(s_1^b - s_1^a)$, and $(s_L^b - s_L^a)$ are all greater than zero, if $\bar{\sigma}_D$ is sufficiently small and/or the absolute value of $m^a(s_1^b - s_1^a)$ is sufficiently large, $Dy^a - Dy^b$ can be negative indicating that group b gains relative to group a.

The reason that this result seems paradoxical is that the intuitive reasoning is based on the partial analysis conclusion that the gross of tax price of the taxed good must rise. When tastes are not identical between the groups, the gross of tax relative price of the taxed good may in fact fall, a result that is consistent with stability. In Figure 2 it was seen that if demand conditions are independent of the redistributive effects of the tax, then the imposition of the tax would raise the gross of tax relative price to $p_B > p_A$. In fact, even if demand conditions are not independent of the tax, the gross of tax relative price may rise as in the cases of D' and D". But if the group prefers the good intensive in "their" factor, it is possible for the redistribution effect due to changes in factor prices to shift the post tax demand curve sufficiently to the left as D'" so that the gross of tax price of the good X_1 falls to p_E. Therefore a group might find its factor income diminished by the tax, but the redistribution shifts demand away from their preferred commodity. This effect could be large enough to lower the gross of tax cost of the pre-tax bundle and thereby offsetting their loss in factor income. It can be seen in Figure 2 that the more inelastic the demand curve (i.e., the steeper is D at a given value of p and X_1), the more likely that this will happen for a given leftward shift of D. Therefore when tastes and factor shares differ, the relative tax incidence among groups cannot be qualitatively ascertained on the basis of "inequality" assumptions such as the factor intensity of the taxed good, the relative commodity preferences and factor shares of the relevant groups.

The preceding has emphasized the qualitative ambiguity of the incidence of a sales tax when both tastes and factor shares differ. However, it can be demonstrated that the expected result will obtain if $\bar{\sigma}_D \geq 1$. Since $m^a(s_1^b - s_1^a)$ is the product of two numbers whose absolute values are smaller than unity, its absolute value must also be smaller than unity so that $\bar{\sigma}_D \geq 1$ will insure that $\bar{\sigma}_D + m^a(s_1^b - s_1^a) > 0$. Then if one of the groups prefers the taxed good and the factor intensive in that good [that is, the two terms $|z|(s_L^b - s_L^a)$ and $(s_1^b - s_1^a)$ have the same sign in expression (1.19)], that group must lose relative to the other group.

Conclusions

The extensions of the two sector model of tax incidence in this chapter can be summarized by two broad conclusions. The first and second order approximations of the incidence of a <u>discrete</u> corporation income tax do not alter Harberger's conclusion that capital tends to bear the burden of the tax. In fact, the second order approximations increase the burden on capital using Harberger's data and assumptions about the elasticities of substitution. The synthesis of commodity and factor price changes in calculating the total general equilibrium incidence of a tax provides a complicated equation for examining the incidence on a particular group. An interesting conclusion from the analysis is that a group which prefers the taxed good and receives a relatively larger share of its income from the factor intensive in that good can be made better off by the tax, i.e., another group can bear over 100 percent of the burden of the sales tax.

CHAPTER II

ON MEASURING WELFARE COSTS IN A GENERAL EQUILIBRIUM MODEL

The basic problem in economics is that of maximizing an objective function subject to a constraint. In the context of an economy with many goods and limited productive resources, constrained maximization requires that certain marginal equalities--the Pareto Optimum conditions--be satisfied. If interpersonal utility comparisons are not possible, these equalities (along with the higher order conditions) determine a maximum only in the sense that they correspond to a point on the utility frontier along which an individual's welfare can only be improved at the expense of someone else. Nevertheless, an important welfare conclusion is obtained, that if the equalities are not satisfied there will be a loss in potential welfare because the satisfaction of the equalities would allow at least one person to be made better off while all others maintain their welfare status.

This chapter examines the problems in measuring the welfare losses resulting from distortions of the efficiency criteria caused by commodity taxes. Before continuing, it will be useful to discuss certain possible misconceptions about welfare changes resulting from such distortions. It is sometimes presumed that these welfare changes are in some way fundamentally different from those resulting from changes in productive capacity such as occurs when the supply of factors or technology of production changes. Specifically, it may be asserted that welfare losses from distortions involve

DOI: 10.4324/9781003167624-3

higher order derivatives of the underlying utility functions whereas other welfare changes do not. This assertion is valid only in the sense that in absence of substitutability between commodities,[1] the Pareto equalities are always satisfied[2] hence market distortions will have no effect on the level of welfare while changes in productive capacity will. The assertion is misleading, however, because it may be incorrectly inferred that the welfare changes resulting from distortions are somehow less "real" than those resulting from changes in productive capacity, or that the latter are "first order" welfare changes while the former are of "second order" small. In point of fact, the welfare changes resulting from either source are fully commensurable and will involve the same properties or derivatives of the utility function when substitution is possible. Since the degree of substitutability between commodities depends on higher derivatives of the utility function,[3] the magnitude of welfare losses resulting from distortions will involve these higher derivatives in a way which welfare changes from productive changes may not.

These points are illustrated in Figure 3 where a commodity tax on good X_1 (tan α equals one plus the tax rate) shifts equilibrium from A to C causing utility to fall from U^a to U^c. The same loss in utility would result if productive capacity fell from that given by the transformation curve

---

[1]Or factors if factor market distortions are being considered.

[2]The marginal rate of substitution between commodities consumed in fixed proportions is indeterminate between zero and infinity at the vertex of the indifference curve, thus any tax between minus and plus infinity leaves the equilibrium unchanged.

[3]For example, the partial elasticity of substitution between X_i and X_j for a homogeneous utility function is $\sigma_{ij} = U_i U_j / U\, U_{ij}$ and thus is inversely related to the second order partial derivative. See R. D. G. Allen, Mathematical Analysis for Economists (London: Macmillan, 1938), p. 343.

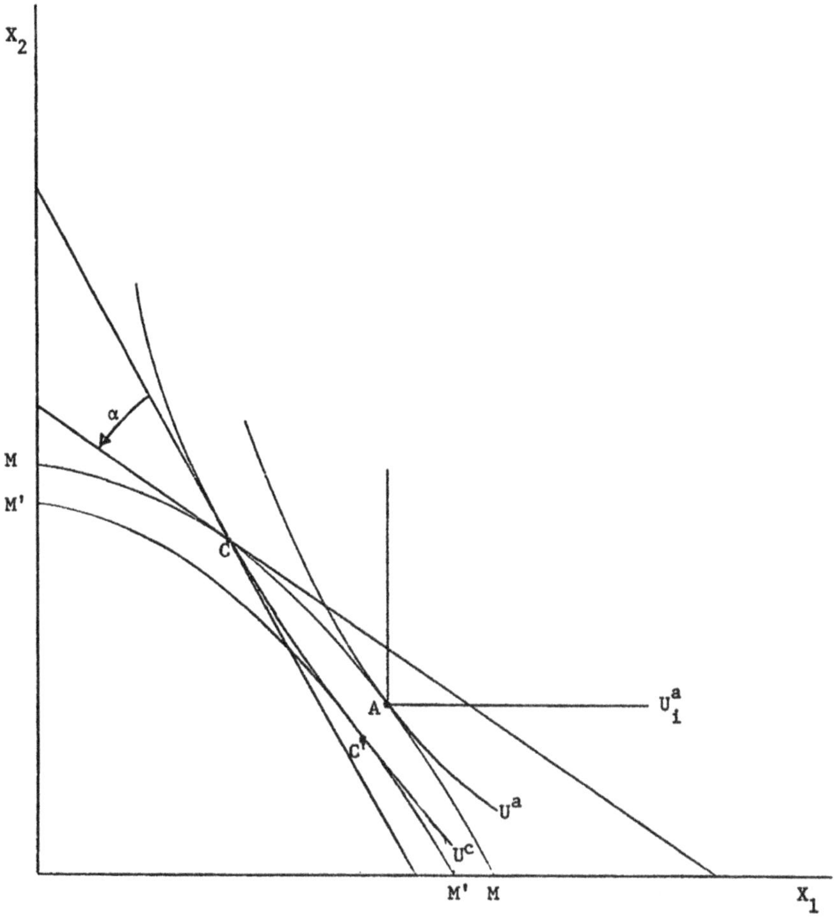

Fig. 3.--A comparison of the effects of a commodity tax and a reduction of productive capacity on welfare.

MM to that by M'M', thus the welfare loss of the distortion cannot be any less "real" than the loss resulting from diminished productive capacity. If the commodities were not substitutable in consumption, the indifference curves would be right angles such as U_f^a and the post tax equilibrium would remain at A and no welfare loss would result from the tax while the shift in the transformation curve would still reduce utility. That is, the presence of demand substitutability is necessary for welfare losses resulting from commodity market distortions while it is not necessary for capacity changes.

This chapter is concerned with the problem of consistently measuring the welfare losses of commodity market distortions, and it should be emphasized that the problems which are analyzed are in no way unique to costs of distortions analysis but are common to any attempt to measure welfare changes when relative prices differ between the situations compared and commodities are substitutable in the consumer's preference function. That is, we are dealing with the "index number problem" although the framework of this chapter is more general than that description usually implies. As stated by Samuelson the central objective of quantity (or price) indexes is

> . . . that of determining merely from price and quantity data which of two situations is higher up on an individual's preference scale.[1]

The impossibility of this objective under general specification is forthwith proved by Samuelson,[2] leaving the unsatisfying task of comparing imperfect indexes. This chapter focuses on the Divisia type index advocated by Hotelling and Harberger among others for measuring the welfare losses resulting from

---

[1]Paul Samuelson, Foundations of Economic Analysis (Cambridge: Harvard University Press, 1947; reprint ed., New York: Atheneum, 1965), p. 146.

[2]Ibid., pp. 154-55.

distortions.[1] This index will be found to rank welfare situations consistently with the underlying utility function in several special cases and may be a useful index even in situations where consistency between it and the utility function cannot be assured. A general equilibrium framework of analysis will now be described and since the problems examined do not directly involve the problem of interpersonal utility comparisons, a single consumer will be assumed throughout.

The Welfare Effects of Commodity Taxation in a General Equilibrium Setting

The consumer maximizes a quasi-concave ordinal utility function U(X) where X is a vector of n commodities subject to his budget constraint

$$\Sigma_i^n P_i X_i = I + T = E \tag{2.1}$$

P_i is the gross of tax relative price of the ith commodity and E, I are expenditure and factor income respectively. $T = \Sigma_i^n t_i p_i X_i$ is the amount of taxes collected which are redistributed back to the consumer as a lump sum payment; p_i, t_i denote the relative producers' (net of tax) price and the ad valorem tax rate on good X_i respectively. All the above are expressed in units of the numeraire commodity X_n which, without loss of generality, will be untaxed.[2] Production is constrained to the convex set

---

[1] H. Hotelling, "The General Welfare in Relation to Problems of Railway and Utility Rates," Econometrica 6 (July 1938):242-69; reprinted in K. J. Arrow and T. Scitovsky, eds., Readings in Welfare Economics (Homewood, Ill.: R. D. Irwin, 1969), pp. 284-308. A. C. Harberger, "Taxation, Resource Allocation and Welfare," in The Role of Direct and Indirect Taxes in the Federal Revenue System (Princeton: Princeton University Press, 1964), pp. 25-75; reprinted in Harberger, Taxation and Welfare, pp. 25-62.

[2] There are only n-1 first order conditions $(U_i/U_n) = p_i(1+t_i)/(1+t_n)$ so no loss of generality but some simplicity will be gained by setting $t_n = 0$.

(2.2) $$\pi(X) \leq 0$$

and producers maximize $\Sigma_i^n p_i X_i$ subject to equation (2.2).[1]

The foregoing allows for a general equilibrium solution yielding equilibrium values X*, P*, p*, I*, E*, and T* for a given vector of commodity taxes t*.[2] [To fix ideas, the solution in a two good economy is shown in Figure 4 where the tax free equilibrium is at A while the equilibrium when X_1 is taxed is at C (where $(1 + t_1^c) = \tan \gamma$). Equilibrium values (X_1^c, X_2^c), $(p_1^c = \tan \alpha,\ p_2^c = 1)$, $(P_1^c = \tan \beta,\ P_2^c = 1)$, $I^c = OI$, $E^c = OE$ and $T^c = IE$, are determined, all in units of X_2.] Under certain conditions the equilibrium corresponding to a given tax vector is unique[3] so that the commodity vector can be written as a function of the tax vector, that is $X^* = X(1 + t^*)$. By substitution we obtain the indirect utility function

(2.3) $$U(X(1+t)) = \psi(1+t)$$

which provides the true change in welfare resulting from changing the tax vector from t^0 to t^1 as $\psi(1 + t^1) - \psi(1 + t^0)$. Since the utility function

---

[1]To obtain another n-1 condition $\pi_i/\pi_n = p_i/p_n$ which along with n-1 conditions $U_i/U_n = P_i/P_n$ and $P_i = p_i(1 + t_i)$ can be solved with equation (2.2) for general equilibrium.

[2]An interior equilibrium lying on the transformation frontier is assumed so that the equality holds in equation (2.2).

[3]This assumes the Jacobian $[\partial X_i/\partial t_j]$ is non-singular. Moreover we require the mapping $t \rightarrow X$ to be univalent otherwise multiple equilibria are possible for a given tax vector. A sufficient condition for global univalence is that the above Jacobian be a P-matrix, that is, all its leading principle minors are positive. This appears to be satisfied if all goods are normal. See D. Gale and H. Nikaido, "The Jacobian Matrix and Global Univalance of Mappings," Mathematische Annalen 159 (1965):81-93.

Also note that $X(k(1+t)) = X(1+t)$ where k is a positive scalar constant since $U_i/U_j = (1+t_i)p_i/(1+t_j)p_j = k(1+t_i)p_i/k(1+t_j)p_j$.

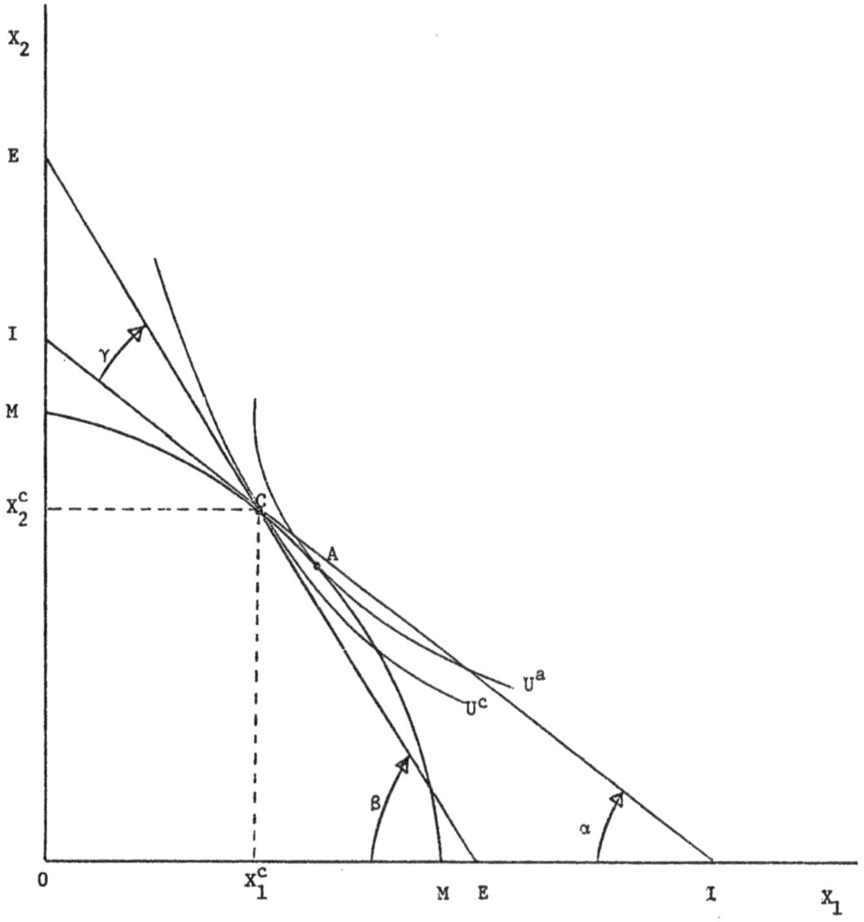

Fig. 4.--Pre- and post-tax general equilibria in a two good economy

is not directly known, we have the general problem of inferring welfare changes from price and quantity data, the main objective in constructing indexes. The convention of measuring welfare costs will be adopted where $WC(t^i, t^j)$ will denote the index of welfare cost (gain if negative) from changing the tax vector from t^j to t^i.

Since the verifiable propositions of consumer demand theory require only an ordinal preference function at most, the actual numerical value of a welfare cost index is of little importance.[1] Therefore it is proposed that welfare cost indexes be evaluated with respect to the following four criteria which I believe exhaust the meaningful properties that an index can possess in view of the fact that the underlying utility function is ordinal.

1. The index should rank any two tax vectors consistently with respect to the underlying utility function. Explicitly,

$$WC(t^j, t^i) \gtreqless 0 \text{ implies that } \psi(t^j) - \psi(t^i) \lesseqgtr 0.$$

A welfare cost index that satisfies this property can rank all possible tax vectors consistently by successive pairwise comparisons. It should be clear that this property is crucial since an index which lacks it would be severely limited in welfare implications.

2. The index should be transitive. That is

$$WC(t^h, t^i) > WC(t^j, t^i) > 0 \text{ implies } \psi(t^h) < \psi(t^j) < \psi(t^i)$$

and vice versa. This would allow the welfare costs of all tax vectors to

---

[1] Except perhaps as a willing to pay interpretation in the cases of the compensating and equivalent variations discussed below in the text.

be ranked by comparing each tax vector to a single initial situation. In practice this property would be important because pairwise comparisons will generally be difficult or impossible. It should be recognized that an index that satisfies (1) does not necessarily satisfy (2), an example being the compensating variation discussed below.

3. The index should be invariant to the order in which the commodity taxes are imposed or changed. This property is important because if an index fails to satisfy it, examples can be constructed for which the index violates properties (1) and (2). This attribute has been the basis for much of the criticism of the Divisia welfare cost index which is a line or surface integral[1] and is not necessarily independent of the path of integration.

4. The index should be capable of being calculated from market data and not require assumptions about the consumer's preference function that cannot be inferred from the data. Any index which requires such knowledge is little better than arbitrarily choosing a utility function in the first place and misses the main objective of index construction. In this category are the Hicksian compensating and equivalent variations which cannot generally be calculated from limited price and quantity data alone.

---

[1]The line or surface integral is more general than the Riemann integral and can be expressed in the form

$$L = \int_{\delta} \Sigma_{i}^{n} F^{i}(X_1, \ldots, X_n)\, dX_i$$

where δ refers to a specific path of the variables $X_1, \ldots, X_n$ in n-space. Any advanced calculus book contains the relevant definitions and theorems of this chapter. A good introduction is H. M. Schey, Div, Grad, Curl and All That (New York: W. W. Norton, 1973). Also R. E. Williamson, R. H. Crowell, and H. F. Trotter, Calculus of Vector Functions (Englewood Cliffs, N.J.: Prentice-Hall, 1968), Chap. 5.

The above properties provide a basis for evaluation of different welfare cost indexes. To begin with, it is well known that the popular fixed-weights indexes such as the Laspeyres and Paasche indexes do not necessarily satisfy properties (1) or (2) although they do satisfy (3) and (4) which accounts for their widespread popularity. Their failure to satisfy properties (1) and (2) has limited their usefulness[1] and provides the impetus for using variable weights indexes as advocated by Divisia.[2] The Divisia index of welfare cost resulting from changing the tax vector from t^0 to t^1 is defined as

$$(2.4) \qquad WC_d = -\Sigma_j^n \int_{t_j^0}^{t_j^1} \Sigma_i^n P_i(t)\ (\partial X_i/\partial t_j)dt_j$$

where $\partial X_i/\partial t_j$ is a general equilibrium substitution term expressing how the equilibrium value of X_i changes when t_j changes. Using $P_i = p_i(1+t_i)$ and noting that since all equilibria are constrained to the transformation surface, $\Sigma_j^n \Sigma_i^n p_i\ (\partial X_i/\partial t_j)dt_j = \Sigma_i^n p_i\ dX_i = 0$, and equation (2.4) can be expressed as the more familiar[3]

$$(2.4') \qquad WC_d = -\Sigma_j^n \int_{t_j^0}^{t_j^1} \Sigma_i^n t_i\ p_i(t)\ (\partial X_i/\partial t_j)dt_j$$

---

[1]However it is well known that together they can indicate whether utility has risen or fallen. The region of ignorance obtains when one index indicates utility has risen and the other that it has fallen.

[2]F. Divisia, Economie Rationnelle (Paris: n.p., 1928).

[3]If the transformation surface is linear then units of the commodities can be set such that all the $p_i = 1$. Then if all taxes are zero except t_j which changes from zero to t_j^* and if the general equilibrium substitution term $\partial X_j/\partial t_j$ is constant, equation (2.4') can be reduced to the familiar triangle equation of Hotelling and Harberger. That is:

$$(2.4'') \qquad WC_d = -\frac{1}{2}(t_j^*)^2\ (\partial X_j/\partial t_j).$$

which is measured in units of the numeraire good since all the relative prices are expressed in that good.

Differential Changes in Commodity Taxes

Utility maximization by the consumer subject to his budget constraint yields the following n-1 first order conditions.

(2.5.1) to (2.5.n-1)
$$R^{in}(X) = \frac{U_i(X)}{U_n(X)} = P_i = p_i(1 + t_i)$$

where $R^{in}(X)$ is the marginal rate of substitution between X_i and the numeraire good X_n. Profit maximization by competitive producers provides for n-1 equations:

(2.6.1) to (2.6.n-1)
$$Z^{in}(X) = \frac{\pi_i(X)}{\pi_n(X)} = p_i$$

where $Z^{in}(X)$ is the marginal rate of transformation between X_i and X_n. The production side can be simplified without loss of generality by assuming that the transformation surface is linear in which case the units of the X_i can be set so that the production constraint (2.2) is

(2.2')
$$\Sigma_1^n X_i - M = 0$$

where M is a constant. In this case all $p_i = 1$ so $P_i = (1 + t_i)$, and general equilibrium is found when equations (2.5) are solved simultaneously with (2.2'). The general equilibrium substitution term can be found by differentiating equations (2.5) and (2.2') and solving for the specific term.[1]

[1]Differentiating (2.5) and (2.2') with respect to t_k we get

The Hicksian compensating variation for a differential change in the tax vector t is obtained as follows. Recalling that E (which is the consumer's disposable income at post tax relative prices) is an endogenous variable depending on t, now let E contain an exogenous component θ which is zero at the initial situation. Component θ can be viewed as a shift parameter since changes in it cause parallel shifts in the post tax budget line (such as EE) in Figure 4. Letting the general equilibrium values associated with tax vector t* be denoted by an asterisk we get $X^*(t^*, E^*(t^*; \theta))$ which is substituted into the utility function to get the indirect utility function $\psi(t^*; \theta) = U(X^*[t^*, E^*(t^*; \theta)])$. Suppressing the asterisk but remembering that we are dealing with equilibrium values we can use

$$\psi_j = \Sigma_i^n U_i \cdot(\partial X_i/\partial t_j); \quad \psi_\theta = \Sigma_i^n U_i \cdot(\partial X_i/\partial \theta) \text{ and } U_i = \lambda(1 + t_i)$$

to obtain

$$\text{(2.7)} \qquad \frac{d\psi}{\lambda} = \Sigma_i^n \Sigma_j^n (1+t_i)(\partial X_i/\partial t_j)dt_j + \Sigma_i^n P_i (\partial X_i/\partial \theta)d\theta$$

where λ is the marginal utility of income, $\partial X_i/\partial t_j$ is the general equilibrium substitution term and $P_i \; \partial X_i/\partial \theta$ is the marginal propensity to consume X_i.

$$\begin{bmatrix} R_1^{1n} & \cdots & R_n^{1n} \\ & \cdots\cdots & \\ R_1^{kn} & \cdots & R_n^{kn} \\ & \cdots\cdots & \\ R^{n-1,n} & & R^{n-1,n} \\ 1 & \cdots & 1 \end{bmatrix} \begin{bmatrix} \partial X_1/\partial t_k \\ \cdot \\ \cdot \\ \cdot \\ \cdot \\ \partial X_n/\partial t_k \end{bmatrix} = \begin{bmatrix} 0 \\ \cdot \\ 1 \\ \cdot \\ \cdot \\ 0 \end{bmatrix}$$

which can be solved for any $\partial X_i/\partial t_k$ assuming the matrix is non-singular. Explicitly, $\partial X_i/\partial t_k = D_{ik}/D$ where D_{ik} is the ik^{th} cofactor and D is the determinant of the matrix respectively.

Recalling that $\Sigma_i^n \Sigma_j^n (\partial X_i/\partial t_j)dt_j = 0$ from equation (2.2') and noting that $\Sigma_i^n P_i(\partial X_i/\partial \theta) = 1$, equation (2.7) becomes

$$\frac{d\psi}{\lambda} = \Sigma_i^n \Sigma_j^n t_i (\partial X_i/\partial t_j)dt_j + d\theta \, . \tag{2.7'}$$

Since the compensating variation is that increment in income at post tax relative prices that will return the consumer to his pre-tax level of utility, it can be obtained by setting $d\theta$ such that $d\psi/\lambda = 0$ which occurs if

$$d\theta = - \Sigma_i^n \Sigma_j^n t_i (\partial X_i/\partial t_j)dt_j \tag{2.7''}$$

which can be recognized as the integrand of equation (2.4') when all $p_i = 1.$[1] By its definition, the differential compensating variation satisfies all properties (1) to (4)[2] therefore differential changes in the commodity tax vector pose no problems for welfare cost measurement beyond estimating $\partial X_i/\partial t_j$. This is not surprising since for differential changes the problem of choosing weights does not arise and the Laspeyres, Paasche, and Divisia indexes all equal the above compensating and equivalent variation.

As is well known, the problems arise when discrete changes are considered, where the Divisia index tries to solve the problem of which weights to choose by summing (integrating) these differential compensating variations. But for discrete changes, the Divisia integral will not in general equal the compensating or equivalent variations, nor will the latter be

---

[1]Because we are dealing with differential changes, expression (2.7") is also equal to the equivalent variation which is defined as the increment by which income must be reduced at pre-tax increment relative prices in order to cause the same loss in utility as caused by the tax increment.

[2]Property (1) is satisfied because $d\theta \gtrless 0$ as $d\psi \lesseqgtr 0$ while (2) holds since if a second differential change in the tax vector dt^2 is considered, it is clear from (2.7") that $d\theta^2 \gtrless d\theta^1$ as $d\psi^2 \lessgtr d\psi^1$; (3) holds since no integration is involved and (4) because only market data are required. It should be noted that as stated above in the text, the compensating variation of a discrete change does not necessarily satisfy property (2) but satisfies (1) and (3).

equal to each other. At this point it should be clear that the problem of consistently measuring the welfare costs of taxes and distortions is nothing more than the search for ideal quantity indexes. Yet in the voluminous literature on this subject, ranging from the concept of consumer's surplus and the constancy of the marginal utility of income to the path dependency of Divisia integrals, this fact does not seem to be explicitly recognized.[1] This point is emphasized since some of the following results are well known in the literature of invariant indexes.[2]

Discrete Tax Changes and the Measurement of Welfare Cost

Although discrete changes in the commodity vector do not pose any problems for the welfare implications of quantity indexes when the relative prices remain unchanged,[3] the index number problem arises if the relative price vector differs between the initial and terminal equilibrium. Moreover, this problem will nearly always arise for discrete changes caused by commodity taxes. In this case, we may be able to infer welfare changes by the revealed preference criteria[4] but a "region of ignorance" always

---

[1]An exception is Samuelson, Foundations, p. 196, where he states "as for its [concept of consumers' surplus] connection with the theory of index numbers, after the concept has been renovated and altered, it *is* simply the economic theory of index numbers . . ."

[2]A recent survey is P. A. Samuelson and S. Swamy, "Invariant Index Numbers and Canonical Duality: Survey and Synthesis," American Economic Review 64 (September 1974):566-93.

[3]By revealed preference, $U(X^1) \gtreqless U(X^0)$ as $\Sigma_i^n \bar{P}_i X_i^1 \gtreqless \Sigma_i^n \bar{P}_i X_i^0$ where $\bar{P}$ is the common price vector. See next footnote.

[4]$U(X^1) > U(X^0)$ if $\Sigma_i^n P_i^1 X_i^1 \geq \Sigma_i^n P_i^1 X_i^0$ and $U(X^1) < U(X^0)$ if $\Sigma_i^n P_i^0 X_i^1 \leq \Sigma_i^n P_i^0 X_i^0$ which includes the two special cases where $X_i^1 \geq X_i^0$ for all i or $X_i^1 \leq X_i^0$ for all i. That is, X^1 has more or less of every commodity than the initial vector X^0.

remains[1] which welfare cost indexes attempt to penetrate. As mentioned, the Divisia index tries to circumvent the problem of choosing weights by treating the discrete change in the commodity and tax vectors as a continuum of differential changes where each differential change is weighted by the relative price vector corresponding to that point, the latter depending on the path of integration. That the Divisia expression is a line or surface integral and may be dependent on the path of integration has been recognized from Hotelling on, but its negative implications have been minimized mainly on the basis that

> . . . there is a good reason to expect these integrability conditions which insure path independency to be satisfied, at least to a close approximation in an extensive number of cases.[2]

In fact, the Divisia index as calculated from market data can be shown to satisfy the integrability conditions only in special cases, and the acceptability of a close approximation is doubtful because any path dependency at all allows examples to be constructed for which the Divisia index does not satisfy property (1). This fact was sufficient for several writers to reject the Divisia welfare cost index and recommend the compensating or equivalent variations.[3] The practicality of this recommendation is disputed in this chapter.

Perhaps the issues can be clarified if the following three demand functions are considered.

---

[1]Samuelson, Foundations, pp. 148-49, and W. E. Diewert, Harberger's Indicator and Revealed Preference Theory, Technical Report #104, The Institute for Mathematical Studies in the Social Sciences (Stanford: Stanford University, 1973), p. 3.

[2]Hotelling, "The General Welfare," p. 247.

[3]E. Silberberg, "Duality and the Many Consumers' Surpluses," American Economic Review 62 (December 1972):942-52, and H. Mohring, "Alternative Welfare Gain and Loss Measures," Western Economic Journal 9 (December 1971):349-68.

1. The partial equilibrium or ceteris paribus demand function obtained by solving the first order conditions (2.5) with the consumer's budget constraint (2.1) where E = I is a constant. This is a money income constant demand function where the tax revenues extracted from the private sector are not returned to it either as a lump-sum payment or as public goods.

2. The constant utility or real income constant demand function obtained by solving equations (2.5) with $U(X) = U^k$ where U^k is some specified level of utility often that corresponding to the initial or terminal situation. This demand function results when the consumer is compensated sufficiently for him to maintain a given level of utility.[1]

3. The general equilibrium demand function is obtained by solving equations (2.5) with the transformation surface equation (2.2) or (2.2'). Presumably it is this demand function that is revealed when a tax is imposed and the revenues are redistributed allowing the consumer to remain on the transformation surface, and it is this demand function to which the Divisia integral corresponds.[2]

Using $dX_i = \Sigma_k^n (\partial X_i/\partial t_j)dt_j$, the Divisia index in equation (2.4) can be written

$$WC_d = - \int_{X^0}^{X^1} \Sigma_i^n P_i(X)dX_i \tag{2.8}$$

---

[1]This is sometimes referred to as the Hicks compensated demand function. Hicks calls it the marginal valuation curve and demonstrates the relationship between specific marginal valuation curves and the compensating and equivalent variations. See J. R. Hicks, A Revision of Demand Theory (Oxford: Clarendon Press, 1959), Chaps. 7 to 10.

[2]This appears to be the implication of Hotelling, "The General Welfare," pp. 249-50 and A. C. Harberger, "Three Basic Postulates for Applied Welfare Economics: An Interpretative Essay," Journal of Economic Literature 9 (September 1971):11-12.

by the usual change of variables technique[1] where X^0 and X^1 are the equilibrium commodity vectors corresponding to t^0 and t^1 respectively. By Stoke's and Green's theorems on line and surface integrals, the necessary and sufficient conditions for (2.8) to be independent of the path of integrations is that[2]

$$\frac{\partial X_i}{\partial P_j} = \frac{\partial X_j}{\partial P_i} \quad \text{for all } i \text{ and } j \tag{2.9}$$

which are generally referred to as the integrability conditions.

The question of the path dependency of the Divisia index resolves to whether or not these conditions are satisfied for the general equilibrium demand function. Some recent critics have based their case on the fact that the constant money income demand function does not generally satisfy these conditions,[3] and Divisia defenders could rightfully assert that they are dealing with "compensated" demand functions. Unfortunately, as demonstrated in Appendix B, under general conditions only the constant utility demand function satisfies (2.9) (on the basis of the symmetry of the Hicks-Slutsky matrix) and that the general equilibrium demand function only

---

[1]Recall that it is assumed that $t \to X$ is a univalent mapping. See n. 3, p. 33, on this point.

[2]Williamson et al., Calculus of Vector Functions, pp. 375-76. In obtaining (2.9) it was assumed that the price-quantity relation was invertible, that is, that $\partial X_i/\partial P_j = (\partial P_j/\partial X_i)^{-1}$. Considerable work has been done in demonstrating that the demand function is integrable (the utility function is recoverable) even if the relation is not invertible because of "kinks" in the indifference surfaces, etc. These considerations are ignored in this chapter but for further reference see L. Hurwicz, "On the Problem of Integrability of Demand Functions," in J. Chipman et al., eds., Preference, Utility and Demand (New York: Harcourt Brace, 1971), see Chap. 9.

[3]Silberberg, "Duality and the Many Consumers' Surpluses," p. 945.

satisfies (2.9) in a small neighborhood around the zero tax equilibrium where the general equilibrium demand function asymptotically approximates (is tangent to) the constant utility demand function.

Thus the path dependency issue can be justifiably raised as an objection to the Divisia index, particularly when it is extolled as an exact measure of welfare changes which is invariant to the specification of the utility function. However, it is not clear that this problem justifies the outright rejection of the Divisia index but rather suggests that the index be examined a little more closely and in the context of the general impossibility of consistently inferring welfare changes from market data alone. In the following sections it will be demonstrated that the Divisia index can be "normalized" so as to make it consistent with certain utility function specifications, in particular when the utility function (1) is homothetic, (2) corresponds to the case of "parallel" indifference surfaces, and (3) is that underlying the so-called linear expenditure functions. In addition, it will be demonstrated that the Divisia index is consistent with any quasi-concave utility function if the economy can be reduced to two (composite) normal goods.

The Divisia Index and Homothetic Utility Functions

It is possible to demonstrate that if the underlying utility function is homothetic the Divisia index can be normalized so as to satisfy all properties (1) to (4). Begin by considering a utility function $H = H(X)$ which is homogeneous of degree $q > 0$. Now following Harberger and Diewert[1]

---

[1] In Harberger, "Three Basic Postulates," pp. 793-94, and Diewert, Harberger's Indicator and Revealed Preference, p. 6, there is the definite implication that the normalization (above) is undertaken to eliminate changes in the nominal unit. In this chapter the normalization is carried

we "normalize" each relative price P_i by dividing it by $E = \Sigma_j^n P_j X_j$ which is income at consumer's prices. Now equation (2.8) becomes

$$\text{(2.8')} \qquad WC_d = - \int_{X^0}^{X^1} \Sigma_i^n \left(\frac{P_i}{\Sigma_j^n P_j X_j}\right) dX_i \, .$$

By equations (2.5) $P_i = H_i(X)/H_n(X)$ and by Euler's theorem $\Sigma_j^n H_j X_j = qH(X)$ so equation (2.8') becomes

$$\text{(2.8")} \qquad WC_d = - q^{-1} \int_{X^0}^{X^1} \Sigma_i^n (H_i(X)/H(X))dX_i = - q^{-1} \int_{X^0}^{X^1} dH(X)/H(X)$$

$$= q^{-1}(\ln H(X^0) - \ln H(X^1))$$

$$\text{or} \quad \exp\{q \cdot WC_d\} = H(X^0)/H(X^1).$$

From equation (2.8") it is easy to show that WC_d now satisfies all the criteria or properties (1) to (4). Property (1) is satisfied because $H(X^0) \gtrless H(X^1)$ implies that $\exp\{q \cdot WC_d(t^1, t^0)\} \gtrless 1$ which implies that $WC_d \gtrless 0$ since $q > 0$. Property (2) is satisfied since $H(X^0) > H(X^1) > H(X^2)$ implies that $\exp\{q \cdot WC_d(t^2, t^0)\} > \exp\{q . WC_d(t^1, t^0)\} > 1$ which in turn implies that $WC_d(t^2, t^0) > WC_d(t^1, t^0) > 0$. Similarly if the inequalities are reversed. Property (3) is satisfied since $P_i(X)/\Sigma_j^n P_j(X)X_j$ must satisfy

---

out even though all values are already expressed in "real" terms by using a numeraire good. The reason is that just any normalization will not do; that is, the problem is more involved than the indeterminacy of the nominal unit. To understand this, it must be realized that finding an ideal price index with which to deflate our nominal values is the dual of the problem of finding the ideal quantity and welfare cost index. The objectives are not independent of each other. On this basis, if the utility function is homothetic the Divisia quantity index will satisfy the desired properties if nominal prices are normalized by dividing by nominal income at consumer's prices or equivalently if numeraire prices (nominal prices/P_n) are divided by numeraire income at consumer's prices (nominal income/P_n). Similarly, by the duality relationship the Divisia price index is exact if quantity weights are normalized by dividing by income at consumer's prices.

the integrability conditions (2.9) since it equals $H_i(X)/H(X)$ which is the gradient vector of the function ln H(X). This fact insures that equation (2.9) holds and the normalized index is path independent.[1] Finally property (4) holds since only market data was used in calculating the normalized Divisia index.

The extension of these results to the more general homothetic utility function is most easily accomplished by noting that a homothetic utility function is a monotonic transformation of a homogeneous function. That is, $U = F(H(X))$ where U is homothetic and $F'(H) > 0$ for all values of H. Now $P_i = F'(H)\cdot H_i/F'(H)\cdot H_n = H_i/H_n$ so WC_d satisfies equation (2.8") as before. But by the monotonicity assumption it is clear that

$$\frac{U(X^0)}{U(X^1)} = \frac{F(H(X^0))}{F(H(X^1))} \gtrless 1 \quad \text{as} \quad \frac{H(X^0)}{H(X^1)} \gtrless 1$$

so all the properties (1) to (4) can be demonstrated to be satisfied by WC_d if U(X) is substituted for H(X).[2]

The Divisia Index, Compensating and Equivalent Variations in a Two Commodity Economy

In this section, the Divisia index is shown to be bound by the compensating and equivalent variations in a two commodity model, and will

---

[1] Williamson et al., Calculus of Vector Functions, Theorem 4.3 on p. 378.

[2] It is interesting to note that homothetic utility functions correspond to Samuelson's "first sense" in which the marginal utility of income can be considered constant, in this case it is independent of the price vector which implies that the elasticity of the marginal utility of income with respect to income is minus unity. P. A. Samuelson, "The Constancy of the Marginal Utility of Income," in The Collected Scientific Papers of Paul A. Samuelson, ed. J. Stiglitz, vol. I (Cambridge, Mass.: M.I.T. Press, 1966), p. 42.

satisfy properties (1) to (4) providing both goods are normal Consider a two good economy with linear transformation curve MM as shown in Figure 5 where commodity units are set such that the slope of MM is -1.[1] The initial equilibrium is at A (where taxes are absent) and the terminal equilibrium is at C where X_1 is taxed at rate t_1^c (or equivalently, X_2 is subsidized) and $U^c < U^a$. The compensating variation is the change in income at post tax increment relative prices that would restore the consumer to his initial level of utility which in Figure 5 is EE' = CC' units of X_2. Note that to find the compensating variation would require complete knowledge of the indifference curve U^a. By inspection of Figure 5 and noting that $U^a = U(X_1, X_2)$ can be solved for $X_2 = \phi^a(X_1)$, the compensating variations can be expressed as the integral

$$(2.10) \qquad CV = - \int_{X_1^a}^{X_1^b} [R(X_1, \phi^a(X_1)) - 1]dX_1 - \int_{X_1^b}^{X_1^c} [R(X_1^b, \phi^a(X_1^b)) - 1]dX_1$$

$$= - \int_{X_1^a}^{X_1^b} [R(X_1, \phi^a(X_1)) - 1]dX_1 - \int_{X_1^b}^{X_1^c} t_1^c \, dX_1$$

where $R(X_1, \phi^a(X_1))$ is the absolute slope of the indifference curve U^a at each value of X_1 and $R(X_1^b, \phi^a(X_1^b)) = 1 + t_1^c$.

The equivalent variation is defined as the amount of income that must be subtracted from the consumer's pre tax increment income to cause the same loss in utility as that resulting from the tax increment, i.e., MM' Note that finding the equivalent variation would require complete knowledge of the indifference curve U^c. Solving $U^c = U(X_1, X_2)$ for $X_2 = \phi^c(X_1)$,

---

[1]Again it is emphasized that this does not involve any loss of generality.

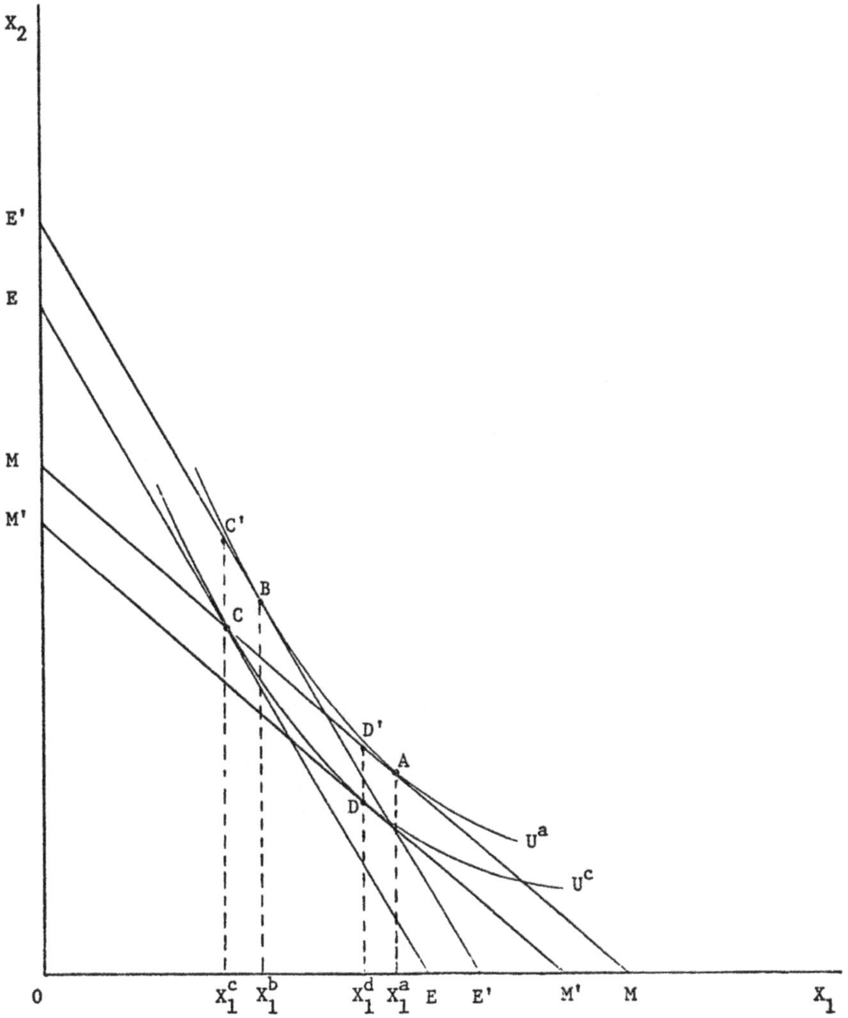

Fig. 5.—The compensating and equivalent variations corresponding to a given commodity market distortion.

the equivalent variation can be expressed as

$$(2.11) \qquad EV = \int_{X_1^c}^{X_1^d} [R(X_1, \phi^c(X_1)) - 1]dX_1 + \int_{X_1^d}^{X_1^a} [R(X_1^d, \phi^c(X_1^d)) - 1]dX_1$$

$$= - \int_{X_1^d}^{X_1^c} [R(X_1, \phi^c(X_1)) - 1]dX_1$$

where $R(X_1, \phi^c(X_1))$ is the absolute slope of the indifference curve U^c at each value of X_1 and noting that $R(X_1^d, \phi^c(X_1^d)) = 1$.

Now consider the Divisia integral in expression (2.8). Using $X_1 + X_2 = M$, $P_1 = 1 + t_1 = R(X_1, M-X_1)$ and $P_2 = 1$, it can be expressed as

$$(2.12) \qquad WC_d(t_1^c, 0) = - \int_{X_1^a}^{X_1^b} [R(X_1, M-X_1) - 1]dX_1 - \int_{X_1^b}^{X_1^c} [R(X_1, M-X_1) - 1]dX_1$$

and

$$(2.12') \qquad WC_d(t_1^c, 0) = - \int_{X_1^a}^{X_1^d} [R(X_1, M-X_1) - 1]dX_1 - \int_{X_1^d}^{X_1^c} [R(X_1, M-X_1) - 1]dX_1$$

where $R(X_1, M-X_1)$ is the absolute slope of the indifference curve intersecting MM at each value of X_1. If the taxed good is normal, then $R(X_1, M-X_1) < R(X_1, \phi^a(X_1))$ for all values of X_1 between X_1^a and X_1^b while $R(X_1, M-X_1) - 1 \leq t_1^c$ for all values of X_1 between X_1^b and X_1^c with the equality holding only at X_1^c. Then by comparing (2.10) with (2.12) it can be seen that $WC_d(t_1^c, 0)$ is less than the compensating variation of CC' units of X_2 provided the taxed good is normal. Conversely it can be shown that $WC_d(t_1^c, 0)$ is greater than the compensating variation when X_1 is inferior. Similarly, by comparing (2.11) to (2.12') it can be shown that $WC_d(t_1^c, 0)$ exceeds the equivalent variation when X_1 is normal and is less than the equivalent variation if it is inferior. This follows since

$R(X_1, M-X_1) > R(X_1, \phi^c(X_1))$ for X_1 between X_1^c and X_1^d while $R(X_1, M-X_1) \geq 0$ for X_1 between X_1^d and X_1^a with the equality holding at X_1^a. Finally, in the special case where the indifference curves in Figure 5 are vertically parallel and X_1 has zero income elasticity, the Divisia index, compensating and equivalent variations are all equal. In this case, $X_1^c = X_1^b$ and $X_1^d = X_1^a$ while $R(X_1, M-X_1) = R(X_1, \phi^a(X_1)) = R(X_1, \phi^c(X_1))$ for all values of X_1 thus equations (2.10) to (2.12') become the same. Note that this special case corresponds to the case where Hicks finds that the Marshallian consumer's surplus concept has an unambiguous interpretation[1] and also to Samuelson's "second sense" in which the marginal utility of income can be considered constant.[2]

From the above we derived the relationship

$$(2.13) \qquad EV \lesseqgtr WC_d \lesseqgtr CV \quad \text{as} \quad \varepsilon_1 \gtreqless 0$$

where ε_1 is the income elasticity of the taxed good. Using (2.13) some important conclusions can be reached regarding the Divisia index in the two commodity case.[3] Since the Divisia index is always bound by the compensating and equivalent variations it must satisfy property (1) and be consistent with the utility function. This result follows from the fact that both the equivalent and compensating variations are positive if

---

[1] J. R. Hicks, Value and Capital (Oxford: Clarendon Press, 1939), p. 38.

[2] Samuelson, "Constancy of the Marginal Utility of Income," p. 47.

[3] Equation (2.13) remains valid if a strictly convex transformation curve replaces linear MM. In equations (2.10) to (2.12'), $Z(X_1, \phi^{\pi}(X_1))$ replaces unity as the absolute slope of the transformation curve where $\pi(X_1, X_2)$ is solved for $X_2 = \phi^{\pi}(X_1)$. This term is common to all the equations and does not change the results.

utility falls and negative if it rises, so WC_d must be likewise. Moreover the Divisia index can be shown to satisfy property (2) by the following argument. Consider another tax or subsidy on X_1 of t_1^e. Then[1]

$$WC_d(t_1^e, 0) = - \int_0^{t_1^e} t_1(\partial X_1/\partial t_1)dt_1 - \int_0^{t_1^c} (\partial X_1/\partial t_1)dt_1 - \int_{t_1^c}^{0} t_1(\partial X_1/\partial t_1)dt_1$$

$$= - \int_{t_1^c}^{t_1^e} t_1(\partial X_1/\partial t_1)dt_1 - \int_0^{t_1^c} t_1(\partial X_1/\partial t_1)dt_1$$

$$= WC_d(t_1^e, t_1^c) + WC_d(t_1^c, 0).$$

By equation (2.13), $WC_d(t_1^e, t_1^c)$ is positive or negative depending on whether the level of utility is lower or higher at t_1^e than t_1^c, therefore $WC_d(t_1^e, 0)$ is greater or less than $WC_d(t_1^c, 0)$ depending on whether t_1^e results in a lower or higher level of utility than t_1^c. In this two good model where all equilibria (and adjustment paths) are constrained to the transformation surface, the Divisia index must also be independent of the path of integration. This should be clear from the observation that there is really only one commodity market distortion in a two good economy, that between the marginal rates of transformation and substitution of the two commodities. Therefore any combination to taxes t_1 and t_2 on goods X_1 and X_2 can be replaced with a single tax-cum-subsidy on X_1 of $t_1' = (t_1 - t_2)/1 + t_2)$, and the Divisia integral involves integration over a single variable and is an ordinary Riemann integral.

The foregoing has demonstrated that the Divisia welfare cost index satisfies all properties (1) to (4) for commodity market distortions in a

---

[1]This proof is based on the path dependency of WC_d so that $\int_0^{t_1^c} = -\int_{t_1^c}^{0}$ which is discussed above.

two good economy. Furthermore, in any situation where the composite good theorem can be applied, the results can be extended to a many commodity economy, for example when taxes are raised (in the same proportion) for a group of commodities while taxes are unchanged (or changed in the same proportion) for all remaining commodities. Unfortunately, unlike many propositions demonstrated in the two good case, the results of this section do not generally extend to the case of three or more goods.

The Problem of Path Dependency with Three or More Goods

A major qualitative difference arises when three or more commodities are taxed differently. In the many good case, the numeraire Divisia index does not generally satisfy the conditions of path independency so that properties (1) or (2) cannot be established. In Figure 6, a linear transformation surface for three goods is illustrated where the units of the commodities are set so that $\partial X_1/\partial X_3 = \partial X_2/\partial X_3 = -1$ along the transformation surface. The initial equilibrium is at point A and the terminal equilibrium is at C after taxes are imposed (or existing taxes changed) on goods X_1 and X_2.[1] Depending on how the taxes are changed there are many possible paths along which the economy might adjust between A and C, with two simple examples being the case where the tax on X_1 is changed before the tax on X_2 resulting in the path labeled δ and the case where the tax on X_2 is changed first resulting in the path labeled γ. Unless the indifference surfaces (which are not drawn) are of a particular shape, there is no reason for the Divisia integral calculated along path δ to

---

[1]Without loss of generality, the numeraire good X_3 is assumed to be untaxed.

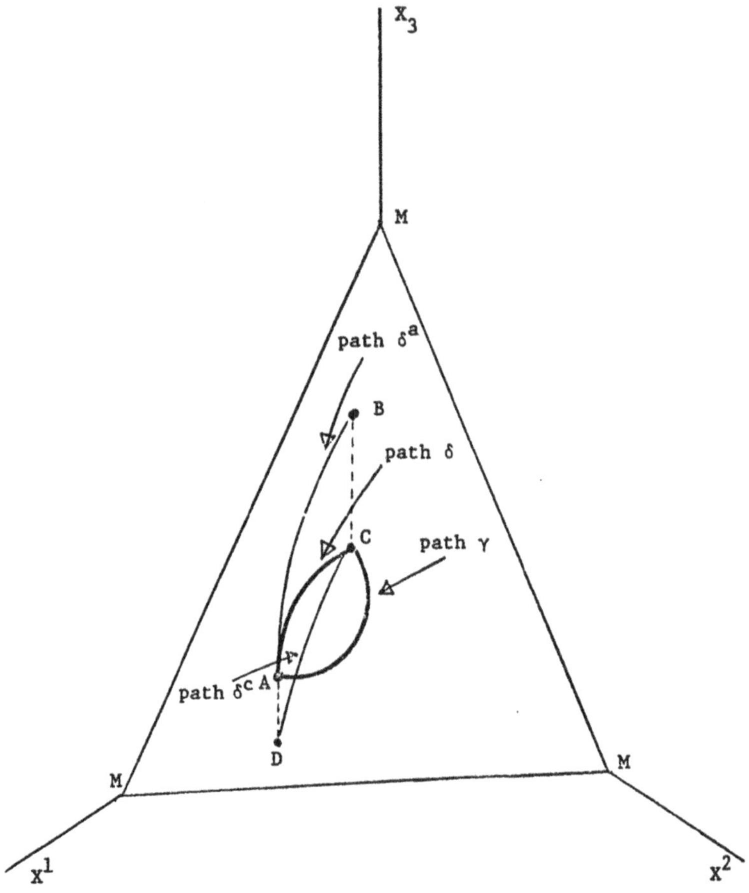

Fig. 6.--The multiple paths on a three good production possibilities surface.

equal that calculated along path γ even though the terminal equilibrium is the same in both cases. Moreover, if taxes are imposed in one order and removed in another, the Divisia integral from A to A along the closed path $\delta \cdot \gamma$ can be non-zero thus contradicting property (1).

In Appendix B it is proven under general conditions that the necessary and sufficient conditions for the Divisia index of welfare cost (where all values are expressed in units of the numeraire good) to be independent of the path of integration is for the marginal utility of the numeraire good (income) to be constant,[1] which means that the indifference surfaces are vertically parallel in Figure 6. That is, the gradient vectors of the indifference surfaces $\{R^{13}(X_1, X_2, X_3), R^{23}(X_1, X_2, X_3), 1\}$ are the same for all indifference surfaces for given values of X_1 and X_2. Equivalently, the marginal propensity to consume the numeraire good is unity at all points so the income expansion path is a vertical line. To understand the sufficiency part of this result, consider any arbitrary path between A and C in Figure 6, for example path δ where the paths δ^a and δ^c are projections of path δ on the indifference surfaces U^a and U^c respectively.[2] Point B lies directly above point C on U^a and the gradient vector at B is the same as at C since the indifference surfaces are parallel. Thus the income plane tangent to U^c at C will be tangent to U^a at B when income is augmented so the compensating variation of moving from A to C is the vertical distance between B and C. Similarly the vertical distance between A and D is the

---

[1]It should be emphasized that these necessary and sufficient conditions apply only to the particular case where all prices are normalized in terms of a numeraire good.

[2]Therefore δ^k is a path such that any point $X_1^\delta, X_2^\delta, X_3^\delta$ on path δ has the corresponding point $X_1^\delta, X_2^\delta, X_3^{\delta k}$ on δ^k where $X_3^{\delta k}$ solves $U^k = U(X_1^\delta, X_2^\delta, X_3^{\delta k})$

equivalent variation which equals the compensating variation since the indifference surfaces are parallel. The compensating variation can be expressed as the following integral:

$$(2.14)\ CV = -\int_{X_1^a}^{X_1^b}[R^{13}(X_1, X_2, \phi^a(X_1, X_2)) - 1]dX_1 - \int_{X_2^a}^{X_2^b}[R^{23}(X_1, X_2, \phi^a(X_1, X_2)) - 1]dX_2$$

which is a line integral along an arbitrary path between A and B, and $U^a = U(X_1, X_2, X_3)$ solves for $X_3 = \phi^a(X_1, X_2)$. Similarly, the equivalent variation can be expressed as the line integral:

$$(2.15)\quad EV = -\int_{X_1^d}^{X_1^c}[R^{13}(X_1, X_2, \phi^c(X_1, X_2)) - 1]dX_1 - \int_{X_2^d}^{X_2^c}[R^{23}(X_1, X_2, \phi^c(X_1, X_2)) - 1]dX_2$$

where $U^c = U(X_1, X_2, X_3)$ is solved for $X_3 = \phi^c(X_1, X_2)$.

The Divisia index of equation (2.8') can be written as

$$(2.16)\ EV = -\int_{X_1^d}^{X_1^c}[R^{13}(X_1, X_2, \phi^c(X_1, X_2)) - 1]dX_1 - \int_{X_2^d}^{X_2^c}[R^{23}(X_1, X_2, \phi^c(X_1, X_2)) - 1]dX_2$$

since $P_i = R^{i3}(X_1, X_2, X_3)$ and $X_1 + X_2 + X_3 = M$ and where the integration is along the path δ. Because the indifference surfaces are vertically parallel, $R^{i3}(X_1, X_2, M-X_1-X_2) = R^{i3}(X_1, X_2, \phi^a(X_1, X_2)) = R^{i3}(X_1, X_2, \phi^c(X_1, X_2))$ and $X_i^a = X_i^d$ and $X_i^c = X_i^b$ for $i = 1, 2$. Therefore equations (2.14) to (2.16) are equal and so are the Divisia index, compensating and equivalent variations. But the compensating and equivalent variations are independent of the paths that expressions (2.14) and (2.15) are integrated along. This should be evident from the fact that the vertical distance between C and B is invariant of the paths used to get to C and B. If this is not convincing then note that $R^{i3}(X_1, X_2, M-X_1-X_2) = R^{i3}(X_1, X_2, \phi^k(X_1, X_2))$ and the latter is an element of the gradient field of a real valued function and must satisfy the integrability conditions $\partial R^{i3}/\partial X_j = \partial R^{j3}/\partial X_i$. This is confirmed by noting that from the definition of $R^{13}(\cdot)$ we get

$$\frac{\partial R^{13}(X_1, X_2, \phi^a(X_1, X_2))}{\partial X_2} = \frac{U_3U_{12} - U_{13}U_2 - U_1U_{32} + U_1U_2U_{33}/U_3}{U_3^2}$$

$$\frac{\partial R^{23}(X_1, X_2, \phi^a(X_1, X_2))}{\partial X_1} = \frac{U_3U_{21} - U_2U_{31} - U_1U_{23} + U_1U_2U_{33}/U_3}{U_3^2}$$

where $\phi_i^a = -U_1/U_3$ by the implicit function theorem.[1] Since $U_{ij} = U_{ji}$ the above expressions are equal so the Divisia index satisfies the integrability conditions and is path independent when the indifference surfaces are parallel. In this case it is also equal to the equivalent variation which is known to satisfy properties (1) and (2) and is therefore consistent with the utility function.

It was demonstrated above that if nominal prices are "normalized" by dividing by P_n (the price of the numeraire good), then the Divisia index will satisfy all properties (1) to (4) including path dependency when the utility function is of the special type where the indifference surfaces are parallel with respect to the numeraire good axis. In a previous section it was demonstrated that the Divisia index satisfies these properties when the utility function is homothetic and nominal prices are "normalized" by dividing by income at consumer's prices, E in nominal units. This clearly begs the question of whether there is always a "normalizing" transformation such that the Divisia index satisfies properties (1) to (4). The answer is yes but it is of little operational significance because knowledge of the

---

[1] Williamson et al., Calculus of Vector Functions, p. 205.

utility function is required to identify the transformation. Formally, the expression $\int \Sigma_i^n P_i(X)dX_i$ can be written as an exact differential equation (and therefore be independent of the path of integration) if there exists an integrating factor $\mu(X)$ such that $G^i(X) = \mu(X)\cdot P_i(X)$ satisfies the integrability conditions $\partial G^i/\partial X_j = \partial G^j/\partial X_i$ for all i and j.[1] It can now be shown that such an integrating factor exists and that it is proportional to the marginal utility of income. That is $\mu(X) = k\lambda(X) = k\lambda(P, E)$ where k is an arbitrary constant and λ is the marginal utility of income. In this case $\mu(X)\cdot P_i(X) = k\,\lambda\,P_i = k\,U_i$ by the first order conditions. Since $U_{ij} = U_{ji}$, the integrating factor satisfies the conditions.

The importance of the two special utility functions considered in this chapter can now be seen. When the utility function is homothetic, it can be demonstrated that $k\lambda = E^{-1}$ where k is an arbitrary constant[2] so normalizing nominal prices by dividing them by E accomplishes the required transformation. Similarly, by the first order conditions, $U_n(X) = \lambda P_n$ where X_n is the numeraire good but when the indifference surfaces are parallel, $U_n(X)$ is a constant. Therefore $k\lambda = p_n^{-1}$ where $k = U_n^{-1}$ so that normalizing nominal prices by dividing them by P_n accomplishes the desired transformation and the numeraire Divisia index satisfies properties (1) to (4) for such a utility function.

Unfortunately, the researcher may be faced with a considerable volume of evidence that the underlying utility function is not homothetic or of the type that yields parallel indifference surfaces since the former implies unitary income elasticities for all goods while the latter implies

---

[1] W. E. Boyce and R. C. DiPrima, Introduction to Differential Equations (New York: Wiley and Sons, 1970), p. 35.

[2] Samuelson, "The Constancy of the Marginal Utility of Income," p. 43.

zero income elasticities for all goods except the numeraire good. It is possible, however, to find utility functions and corresponding transformations of the Divisia index which is not so contradictory of the evidence. For example, the utility function underlying linear expenditure systems which is of the form:

$$(2.17) \qquad U = (X_1 - S_1)^{m_1}(X_2 - S_2)^{m_2} \ldots (X_n - S_n)^{m_n}$$

$$= \pi_i^n (X_i - S_i)^{m_i}$$

where m_i is the marginal propensity to consume X_i and is constant. The S_i are constants and are often interpreted as subsistence levels of consumption of the good X_i. This utility function implies linear demand functions of the form

$$(2.18) \qquad X_i = \Sigma_j^n a_{ij} (P_j/P_i) + m_i (E/P_i)$$

where $a_{ii} = S_i(1 - m_i)$ and $a_{ij} = -m_i S_j$.[1] The empirical implications of this utility function include linear Engles curves passing through the point $\{S_1, S_2, \ldots, S_n\}$ which may be objectional[2] on the basis of existing evidence although it could be assumed that the actual utility function only approximates expression (2.17) in the relevant region and can differ elsewhere.

More importantly for our analysis, it is seen from the first order conditions that

---

[1]H. A. John Green, Consumer Theory (Middlesex, Eng.: Penquin, 1971), pp. 136-37 and 314-18.

[2]P. A. Samuelson, "Some Implications of 'Linearity,'" in The Collected Scientific Papers of Paul A. Samuelson, ed. J. Stiglitz, vol. I (Cambridge: M.I.T. Press, 1966), p. 61.

$$U_i(X) = \frac{m_i U}{X_i - S_i} = \lambda P_i$$

and using $\Sigma_i^n m_i = 1$ we can solve for $\lambda = kP_1^{-m_1} \cdot P_2^{-m_2} \ . \ . \ . \ P_n^{-m_n}$, where $k = \pi_i^n m_i^{m_i}$. Thus normalizing nominal prices in the Divisia index by dividing by $\pi_i^n P_i^{m_i}$ results in $- \int \Sigma_i^n P_i(X)dX_i = -k^{-1} \int \Sigma_i^n U_i(X)dX_i = -k^{-1} \int dU$ where U is of the form in equation (2.17). Admittedly, the Divisia index is still only exact assuming an explicit utility function underlies the market data, but at least it does not require the assumption of a utility function which is blatantly contradicted by the evidence. Undoubtedly, normalizations could be found for more complex, and less empirically confining utility functions such as the translog but the linearity of most empirical work indicates that this is unlikely to be necessary.

Conclusions

Critics of the Divisia index have suggested that the path dependency of this line integral is a serious drawback and that the index should be rejected in favor of the path independent compensating or equivalent variations. If these measures were a practical alternative this would probably end the issue. Unfortunately, while the compensating and equivalent variations are interesting concepts, they do not solve the index number problem for us. Without an explicit specification of the indifference map there is no way to find points such as B and D in Figures 5 and 6 which are needed to calculate these values, and making arbitrary assumptions in order to calculate these points defeats the central objective of constructing index numbers in the first place, which is to make welfare inferences from market data alone.

In this chapter it was demonstrated that the Divisia index can be used to rank welfare situations consistently with respect to the underlying utility function in certain special cases if it is appropriately normalized. If the utility function is that which yields parallel indifference surfaces, the Divisia index can be made exact by normalizing nominal prices by dividing them by the price of the numeraire good. If the utility function is homothetic, then normalizing nominal prices by dividing them by nominal income at consumer's prices will accomplish the desired result. If the zero and unitary income elasticities implies by these utility functions are objectional, the Divisia index can be made exact by normalizing all nominal prices by $\pi_i^n P_i^{m_i}$ if the utility function is of the form in equation (2.17). In this case, the researcher can introduce any non-negative values for the marginal propensities to consume the goods that he wishes. In addition it was demonstrated that the Divisia index satisfies all requirements for consistency with any underlying utility function if the economy can be reduced to two normal composite commodities.

Finally, it should be re-emphasized that if the utility function is unspecified, the Divisia index is path dependent in the multi-good case and welfare implications based on it may be in error. But the Divisia index can be chosen with the knowledge that a universally consistent alternative does not exist and that in the set of imperfect indexes, the Divisia index and the consumer's surplus reasoning underlying it have convenient and useful properties.

CHAPTER III

TRADE AND TRADE TAXES IN AN INTER-TEMPORALLY OPTIMIZING ECONOMY

The two sector optimum growth model developed by Uzawa[1] has proven very useful in analyzing the properties (particularly steady state properties) of inter-temporally optimizing economies. The model has been extended by Bardhan[2] and Ryder,[3] among others, to open economies in order to examine patterns of trade and production along optimal paths of capital accumulation. In this chapter I present some further results about trade and trade taxes in such an economy. Also, a useful diagrammatic interpretation of optimal steady states is presented which is a little richer in intuitive appeal than the state-costate diagrams that usually accompany the optimal growth literature.

Throughout most of the analysis, the country is assumed to face variable terms of trade in the form of an offer curve of the usual configuration. This assumption permits us to avoid certain specialization problems that occur in the case of fixed terms of trade. The opening of trade

---

[1]H. Uzawa, "Optimal Growth in a Two Sector Model of Capital Accumulation," Review of Economic Studies 31 (February 1964):7-24.

[2]P. K. Bardhan, "Optimum Capital Accumulation and International Trade," Review of Economic Studies 32 (July 1965):241-44.

[3]Harl E. Ryder, "Optimal Accumulation and Trade in an Open Economy of Moderate Size," in Essays on the Theory of Optimal Growth, ed. K. Shell (Cambridge: M.I.T. Press, 1967), pp. 7-24.

DOI: 10.4324/9781003167624-4

subject to variable terms of trade will be shown to raise or lower the optimal steady state capital stock depending on whether the country has a comparative advantage in the capital or labor intensive commodity. In the former case, the opening of trade is shown to raise the steady state level of consumption per worker while in the latter, the effect on steady state consumption is ambiguous. These results are invariant as to whether consumption or investment goods are assumed to be capital intensive. In the next section, the effects of free trade on the "golden rule" steady state values are considered. Under free trade, the golden rule does not maximize steady state consumption per worker because of the terms of trade effects, although the golden rule is shown to be re-established if the economy imposes an optimal trade tax. An interesting implication of the results of this section is the possibility of a second best capital tax. In the next section, the effects of incremental changes in trade taxes on steady state values are analyzed. An increase in trade taxes is found to raise or lower the optimal steady state capital stock depending on whether the importable is capital or labor intensive. The effect of increasing trade taxes on steady state consumption is more complicated except for variations of the tax around its optimal value. In this case, an increase in trade taxes raises or lowers steady state consumption depending on whether the importable is capital or labor intensive. The optimal trade policy for an inter-temporally optimizing economy facing variable terms of trade is then examined. The optimal trade tax is shown to be the same as in the conventional static economy. Finally, the case of a small inter-temporally optimizing economy facing fixed world prices is analyzed. The general results of the former sections are found to hold except that production specialization or indeterminacy is possible for the small open economy.

General Equilibrium in an Intertemporally Optimizing Economy

As mentioned, the analytic framework of this chapter is the Uzawa two sector model. I will abstract from exogenous exponential labor force growth and/or labor augmenting technological change since their inclusion would not add anything meaningful to the analysis or results.[1] Investment and consumption goods are costlessly traded when the economy is opened but they may be subject to trade taxes where specified. Investment goods become internationally immobile once they are "bolted down" into the capital stock of a country.

A single price taking consumer (or policy maker) is assumed to maximize

$$V = \int_0^\infty u(c(\tau))e^{-\rho\tau}\, d\tau \tag{3.1}$$

subject to:

$$p\,c + i - r\,k - w - \gamma = 0 \tag{3.2}$$

$$\dot{k} = i - \delta\, k\,. \tag{3.3}$$

Equation (3.1) is the objective functional where $u(\cdot)$ is a utility function with $u'(\cdot) > 0$, $u''(\cdot) < 0$ and $u'(0) = \infty$ and $c(\tau)$ is consumption per worker at time τ. ρ is a positive and constant rate of time preference. Equation (3.2) is the consumer's budget constraint where p is the domestic price of consumption goods in terms of investment goods such that

$$p = p_c^w(1 + t_c)^{-1} \quad \text{and} \quad 1 = p_i^w(1 + t_i)$$

---

[1] In addition, it allows us to avoid the problems of different rates of exponential growth in the domestic country and the rest of the world.

when the goods are traded internationally where the world prices of consumption and investment goods are p_c^w and p_i^w respectively. If investment goods are imported then $t_i > 0$ is an import tariff and $t_c > 0$ is an export tax while if consumption goods are imported, $t_i < 0$ is an export tax and $t_c < 0$ is an import tariff; r and w are the relative prices of capital's and labor's services expressed in units of investment goods (hence r is a pure number), i is gross domestic investment per worker, k is capital stock per worker and γ is a lump sum transfer of the collected tax proceeds. All variables depend on τ but this time dependency is suppressed except where it is needed for clarity. Equation (3.3) is the equation of motion for k where a dot above any variable denotes its rate of change with respect to time. Since the labor force is constant, the level of a variable and its level per worker are used interchangeably.

The optimizing behavior of the consumer is found by forming the Hamiltonian

$$H = u(c) + q[(r - \delta)\, k + w + \gamma - p\, c] \tag{3.4}$$

where q is the costate or auxiliary variable which can be interpreted as the present value (in utils) of a marginal unit of capital. Applying the maximum principle, the first order conditions are:[1]

$$u'(c) - q\, p = 0 \tag{3.5}$$

$$\dot{q} = q(\rho + \delta - r) \tag{3.6}$$

$$\dot{k} = i - \delta\, k \tag{3.3}$$

---

[1]Where $\partial H/\partial c = 0$, $-\partial H/\partial k = \dot{q} - \rho\, q$ and $\partial H/\partial q = \dot{k}$ give equations (3.5), (3.6) and (3.3) respectively.

(3.7) $$k_0 = k(\tau = 0) \text{ and } \lim_{\tau\to\infty} q(\tau)\, k(\tau) = 0,\ \lim_{\tau\to\infty} q(\tau) \geq 0$$

where the equations in (3.7) are the initial and terminal (transversality) conditions.

The production side of the economy is characterized by linear homogeneous production functions, a fixed labor force and competitive producers who maximize net profits

(3.8) $$R = p\, y_c + y_i - rk - w$$

subject to:

(3.9a) $$y_c = \frac{k - k_i}{k_c - k_i}\, f_c(k_c)$$

(3.9b) $$y_i = \frac{k_c - k}{k_c - k_i}\, f_i(k_i) \quad \text{where} \quad k_c \neq k_i .$$

In these equations, y_j is the output of the jth good per worker and k_j, $f_j(k_j)$ are the capital-labor and output-labor ratios in the jth sector respectively. Factor intensity reversals are ruled out and the Inada conditions are assumed to hold.[1] Profit maximization by competitive producers provides:

(3.10) $$f_i'(k_i) = p\, f_c'(k_c)$$

(3.11) $$f_i'(k_i) = r \text{ and } f_i(k_i) - f_i'(k_i)k_i = w$$

---

[1]These are the conditions $f_i'(k_i) > 0$ and $f_i'(0) = \infty$, $f_i'(\infty) = 0$ which insure a positive and finite steady state value of k. See K. Inada, "On a Two Sector Model of Economic Growth: Comments and a Generalization," Review of Economic Studies 31 (April 1964):119-27 and K. Inada, "On the Stability of Growth Equilibrium in Two Sector Models," Review of Economic Studies 31 (April 1964):127-42.

$$(3.12) \qquad \frac{f_i(k_i)}{f_i'(k_i)} - k_i = \frac{f_c(k_c)}{f_c'(k_c)} - k_c$$

where $f_j'(k_j)$ is the marginal product of capital in producing the jth good. Finally, competition insures that net profits R in equation (3.8) equal zero.

The model is completed in a closed (autarky) economy with the conditions

$$(3.13) \qquad y_c = c \quad \text{and} \quad y_i = i.$$

For an open economy, the model is completed by

$$(3.14) \qquad i - y_i = F(c - y_c)$$

$$(3.15) \qquad F(c-y_c) + \pi(c-y_c) = 0$$

where equation (3.14) is a foreign offer curve with $F'(\cdot)$ and $F''(\cdot) < 0$[1] yielding a concave offer curve of the usual configuration shown as FF in Figure 7. In a later section, the case of an economy facing fixed terms of trade is considered. In the present case, equation (3.15) is the condition that trade balance at world prices where $\pi = p_c^w/p_i^w$ is the relative price of consumption goods in world markets. Then trade provides that

$$(3.16) \qquad p(1 + t_c)(1 + t_i) = \pi = -F(c-y_c)/(c-y_c).$$

---

[1]A problem of choosing an offer curve of this kind is that it is inconsistent with the rest of the world as a single inter-temporally optimizing country at its steady state since in this case its offer curve would be infinitely elastic up to the specialization points. The offer curve of equation (3.14) could be explained by assuming that the other country is not inter-temporally optimizing or perhaps consuming both commodities. It might also be derived by assuming that there are a large number of other countries each with a different rate of time preference and distributed so as to produce FF.

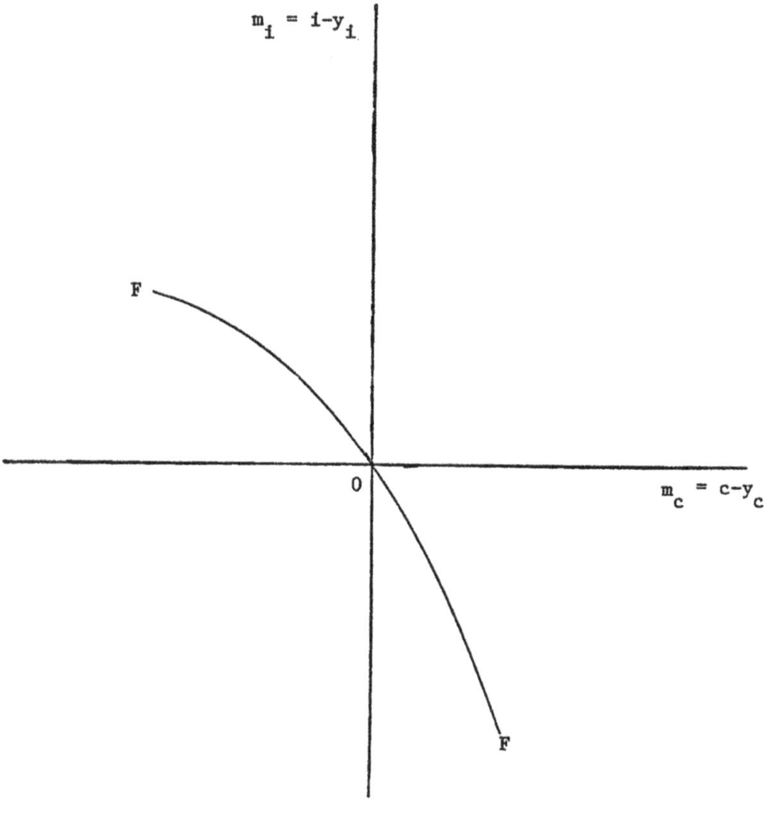

Fig. 7.--The foreign offer curve

Since t_i and t_c enter equation (3.16) (and no others) in the same way, it is clear that the Lerner symmetry[1] (or more correctly, equivalence) theorem between import tariffs and export taxes applies in this model[2] so the term $(1 + t_c)(1 + t_i)$ is replaced with the term $(1 + t)$ and equation (3.16) becomes

$$p(1 + t) = -F(c-y_c)/(c-y_c) \tag{3.16'}$$

where a tax on trade requires that $t > 0$ if investment goods are imported and $t < 0$ if consumption goods are imported.

Perfect foresight general equilibrium solutions exist for the closed and open economies when the optimizing equations of the consumer and producers are realized simultaneously. It is well known that the path of capital accumulation so determined converges to a steady state where

$$i = \delta\, k \tag{3.17}$$

$$f_i'(k_i) = \rho + \delta. \tag{3.18}$$

Equations (3.17) and (3.18) are the steady state conditions for k and q respectively and are obtained by setting $\dot{k} = \dot{q} = 0$ in equations (3.3) and (3.6) and using equation (3.11).

The Opening of Trade in a Moderate Sized Economy

Consider first the country in an autarky state where equation (3.13)

---

[1] A. P. Lerner, "The Symmetry Between Import and Export Taxes," Economica 3 (August 1936):306-13.

[2] This is not a trivial conclusion. Many tax-subsidy equivalences that obtain in an ordinary two good model do not apply in the investment-consumption good model. For example, in a closed economy, a tax on investment goods is not equivalent to a subsidy on consumption goods since the former involves an inter-temporal distortion while the latter does not.

obtains so y_c and c, and y_i and i can be used interchangeably. The perfect foresight general equilibrium steady state is found when equations (3.17) and (3.18) are simultaneously realized. Solving (3.17) along with the optimizing equations of the producers defines a Johnson type "investment requirements" curve[1] for the closed economy and shown as I_r in Figure 8. This I_r curve represents the sustainable levels of consumption per worker possible when investment equals depreciation (i.e., $\dot{k} = 0$), therefore the optimal steady state must lie somewhere on it. The geometric derivation of I_r is rather simple. At every value of k, for example k_a, the production efficiency conditions define a transformation curve such as T_aT_a in Figure 8. Finding the point A on T_aT_a where $i_a = \delta k_a$ gives a single point of I_r, with the I_r curve being the locus of points such as A as k is varied from zero to infinity. Since $k = i/\delta$ along I_r, k could also be measured along the vertical axis of Figure 8 with k increasing for upward movements along I_r.

In Appendix C, various properties of I_r are derived. Its slope is given by

$$(3.19) \qquad \left.\frac{di}{dc}\right|_{I_r} = \frac{\delta\, p}{f_i'(k_i) - \delta} \gtrless 0 \quad \text{as} \quad f_i'(k_i) \gtrless \delta$$

from equation (C.8) of the appendix. As will be shown, $f_i'(k_i)$ declines as k increases along I_r thus I_r is positively sloped for low values of k becoming negatively sloped for high values of k. Maximum sustainable consumption is reached at point G, the so-called golden rule point where $f_i'(k_i) = \delta$. If $\rho \geq 0$ then the optimum steady state must lie on or below point G by the

---

[1]H. G. Johnson, "Trade and Growth: A Geometrical Exposition," Journal of International Economics 1 (February 1971):83-101.

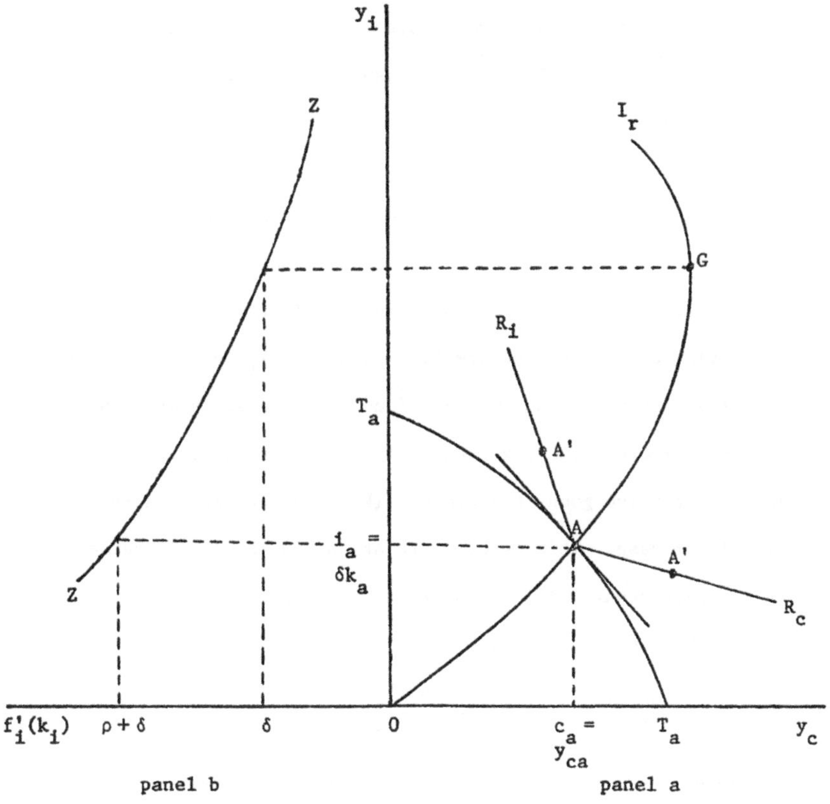

Fig. 8.--The investment requirements and the ZZ loci in a closed economy

Koopman criterion.[1] In fact, since we have assumed that $\rho > 0$, the optimum steady state will lie below G in the positively sloped region of I_r, this point sometimes being referred to as the modified golden rule.

To find the optimum steady state it is first necessary to demonstrate that $f_i'(k_i)$ and the price of the capital intensive good decline as k increases along I_r. Therefore p rises or falls as you move outwards along I_r depending on whether the consumption good is labor or capital intensive. These propositions are proved algebraically in Appendix C but can be established geometrically with reference to Figure 8. Through point A are drawn Rybczynski lines R_iA and R_cA corresponding to capital intensive investment and consumption goods respectively. At constant p, an increase in k shifts production to A'; on R_iA or R_cA depending on which good is capital intensive. By drawing the transformation curve through A' in each case, it is easily seen that p, which equals the absolute slope of the transformation curve, must be greater above A on I_r when investment goods are capital intensive and smaller if consumption goods are capital intensive. Furthermore, $f_i'(k_i)$ varies positively with the relative price of the capital intensive good, therefore $f_i'(k_i)$ declines as k increases along I_r in either case. This negative relationship is plotted between $f_i'(k_i)$ and i (which equals k/δ) as the ZZ curve in panel b of Figure 8. Algebraically, the slope of ZZ is:

$$(3.20) \qquad \left.\frac{di}{d(f_i')}\right|_{I_r} = \frac{-\delta\ p\ A\ (k_c - k_i)}{f_i''(w + \delta\ k_c + (f_i' - \delta)k_i)} < 0$$

---

[1]Any path converging to a steady state lying above G on I_r must be inferior to a path converging to G since the latter allows consumption to be greater at all values of τ and $u'(\cdot) > 0$. See T. C. Koopmans, "On the Concept of Optimal Economic Growth," in Semaine d'Etude sur le Rôle de l'Analyse Econométrique dans la Formulation de Plans de Developpement (Vatican City: Pontifical Academy of Science, 1965).

from equation (C.10) of Appendix C. Its negativity is guaranteed when $f_i'(k_i) > \delta$ (the relevant and positive segment of I_r) because $A \lessgtr 0$ as $k_c \gtrless k_i$ from equation (C.4) in Appendix C, hence $A(k_c - k_i) < 0$. Also $f_i''(k_i) < 0$.

The optimal steady state is found when equation (3.18) obtains which is shown in Figure 8 to occur at point A on I_r with steady state values c_a and $i_a = \delta\, k_a$. For the steady state capital stock k_a can be drawn the transformation curve T_aT_a and the absolute slope of T_aT_a at point A yields the optimal steady state value of p.

Now consider the opening of free trade subject to the offer curve (3.14) and balance of trade condition (3.16') for which $t = 0$. Since the country faces variable terms of trade and the price taking consumer and producers do not exploit this monopsony/monopoly power there is scope for optimal trade intervention, but this possibility is deferred until later in the chapter. To analyze the effects of the opening of free trade on the steady state, equations (3.14), (3.16') and (3.17) are solved along with the production efficiency equations to derive the free trade investment requirements curve shown as I_{rT} in Figure 9. In this diagram, I_{rT} is drawn with respect to i and c on the axes and represents the levels of sustainable consumption that are possible under free trade. As will be seen, I_{rT} must lie to the right of I_r except at a point of tangency labeled N. This results from the expanded consumption and investment opportunities made possible with trade. The geometric derivation of I_{rT} is as follows. Each value of k, such as k_a, allows the determination of a Baldwin free trade envelope curve[1] B_aB_a corresponding to T_aT_a by using equations (3.14)

[1]R. E. Baldwin, "The New Welfare Economics and Gains in International Trade," Quarterly Journal of Economics 66 (February 1952):91-101.

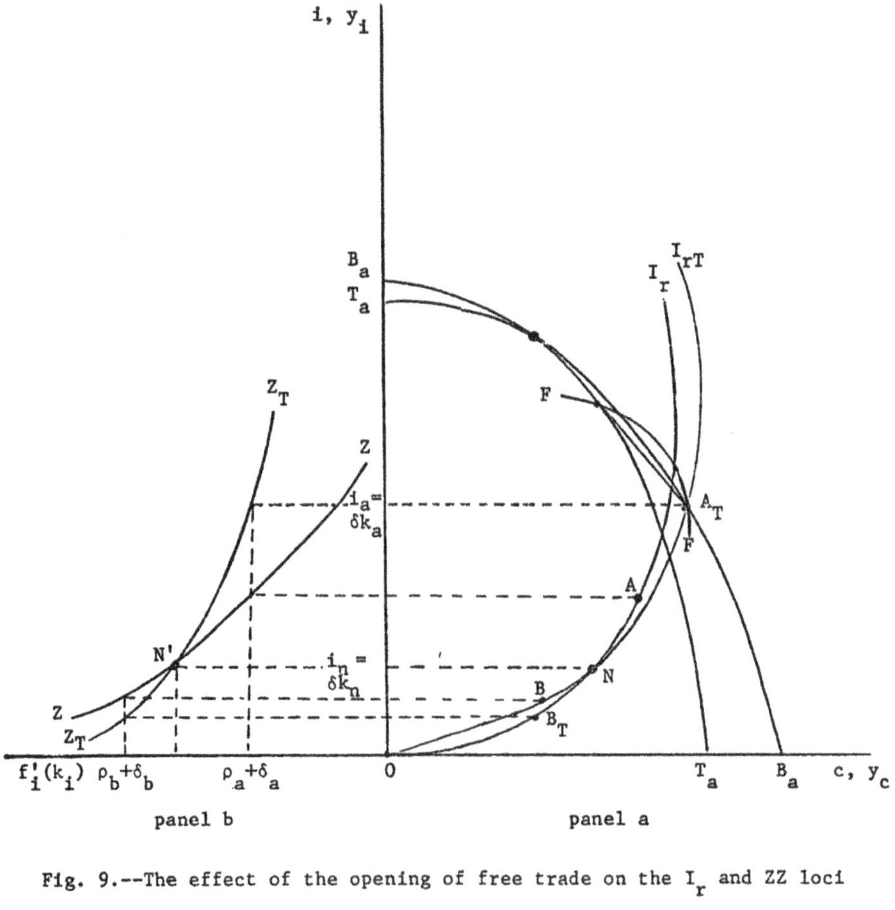

Fig. 9.--The effect of the opening of free trade on the I_r and ZZ loci

and (3.16'). Note that the Baldwin curve is drawn with respect to c and i on the axes while the transformation curve is drawn with respect to y_c and y_i. Point A_T on I_{rT} where $i_a = \delta k_a$ is a point on the I_{rT} curve which is derived by varying k from zero to infinity. Since the Baldwin curve lies outside of the transformation curve (except for a point of tangency) the I_{rT} locus lies to the right of I_r except at a point of tangency which occurs when $k = k_n$ which yields transformation and Baldwin curves which are tangent at the point $i_n = \delta k_n$. At this point, the domestic p in autarky just equals the absolute slope of FF at the origin so the opening of trade provides no inducement for (or gains from) engaging in trade.

A difficult proposition to demonstrate is that a given increase or decrease in steady state k will cause a larger decrease or increase in the marginal product of capital under trade. That is, the return to capital declines more rapidly along I_{rT} than along I_r which is shown as the more steeply sloped Z_TZ_T line drawn between $f_i'(k_i)$ and i in panel b of Figure 9. Z_TZ_T intersects ZZ at N' which corresponds to point N in panel a. The algebraic slope of Z_TZ_T is

$$(3.21) \qquad \left.\frac{di}{d(f_i')}\right|_{I_{rT}} = \frac{-\delta pA(k_c - k_i)}{f_i''(w + \delta k_c + (f_i' - \delta)k_i)} + \frac{F'(\cdot)\delta(m_c(k_c - k_i)^2}{f_c(F - m_cF')(w + \delta k_c + (f_i' - \delta)k_i)}$$

from equation (C.21) of Appendix C. The first term is the slope of ZZ as given by equation (3.20) while the second term is negative when $f_i'(k_i) > \delta$. This follows since $F'(m_c) < 0$, $F(m_c) - m_cF'(m_c) > 0$ by the concavity of F and all remaining terms are positive; m_c equals $c-y_c$ and is imports (if positive) or exports (if negative) of consumption goods.

Thus the (negative) slope of Z_TZ_T is steeper than (less than) the slope of ZZ. This result is also intuitively clear since for values of

$k > k_n$ the country has a comparative advantage in capital intensive goods so the opening of free trade would shift productive towards these commodities raising the marginal product of capital. Hence $Z_T Z_T$ lies to the left of ZZ above point N'. Similarly, for $k < k_n$, the country has a comparative advantage in the labor intensive good so the opening of trade lowers the marginal product of capital at every value of $k < k_n$ and $Z_T Z_T$ lies to the right of ZZ below N'.

The effect of the opening of free trade on steady state values of k and c is shown in Figure 9. If $\rho + \delta = \rho_a + \delta_a$ with the autarky steady state at point A above point N, the opening of trade shifts production towards the capital intensive commodity raising the marginal product of capital above $\rho_a + \delta_a$ at the existing steady state capital stock. Since the return to capital is raised in terms of both commodities, future consumption is made cheaper relative to present consumption and the consumer is induced to accumulate a larger stock of capital. In addition, the steady state consumption level is raised at each value of k (except k_n) because of the gains from trade. Therefore the optimal steady state under free trade lies at point A_T at which both the steady state capital stock and level of consumption is greater than under autarky. If $\rho + \delta = \rho_b + \delta_b$ such that the autarky steady state is at B, the opening of trade shifts production towards the labor intensive commodity lowering the marginal product of capital below $\rho_b + \delta_b$ at the existing steady state capital stock. The consumer is induced to decumulate his capital stock since future consumption is now relatively more expensive as compared to present consumption, therefore after the opening of trade the optimal steady state capital stock is smaller. However, the effect of the opening of trade on steady state consumption is ambiguous since the consumer can enjoy a higher level of consumption with a smaller capital stock because of the expanded consumption opportunities at each value of k made possible by trade. The case of a smaller capital stock and larger steady state consumption is illustrated in Figure 9 where the free trade steady state occurs at B_T.

The results of this section are summarized in the following proposition.

Proposition 1. The opening of free trade raises the optimal steady state capital stock and level of consumption per worker if the country has a comparative advantage in the capital intensive good. If a country's comparative advantage lies in the labor intensive good, the opening of trade will lower the optimal steady state capital stock but may raise or lower the steady state level of consumption per worker.

Free Trade and the Golden Rule

The golden rule of capital accumulation states that sustainable consumption per worker is maximized when $f_i'(k_i) = \delta$.[1] This result is easily derived in the case of a closed economy by setting

$$\frac{dc}{dk} = \frac{dc}{di} \cdot \frac{di}{dk} = \frac{f_i'(k_i) - \delta}{p} = 0 \tag{3.22}$$

where $dc/di = (di/dc)^{-1}$ from equation (3.19) and $di/dk = \delta$ from equation (3.17). Therefore steady state consumption per worker reaches a maximum when the marginal product of capital (in terms of investment goods) equals the exponential rate of capital depreciation, i.e., $f_i'(k_i) = \delta$,[2] shown as point G

[1]The golden rule is conventionally stated as setting the marginal product of capital equal to the exponential rate of growth of the labor force where there is no capital depreciation. The above is an equivalent expression for the case of constant labor force and exponential capital depreciation.

[2]The second order conditions for a maximum are satisfied since $f_i''(k_i) < 0$.

on I_r in Figure 8. It can be demonstrated that this rule does not yield the point of maximum steady state consumption for an economy engaging in free trade and facing variable terms of trade.

In Appendix C, the slope of the free trade investment requirements curve is given by

$$\text{(3.23)} \qquad \left.\frac{di}{dc}\right|_{I_{rT}} = \frac{-\beta\delta}{f_i'(k_i) + \theta - \delta}$$

from equation (C.16) of Appendix C, where β is shown to be negative in equation (C.17) and can be interpreted as the slope of the free trade Baldwin envelope curve passing through that point on I_{rT}. The term θ in the denominator of (3.23) is equal to

$$\text{(3.24)} \qquad \theta = \frac{m_c f_c f_i''(k_i)}{Af_c + \dfrac{f_i''(k_i)\, m_c^2 (k_c - k_i)}{F(m_c) - m_c F'(m_c)}}$$

from equation (C.18) in Appendix C. It can be established that $\theta \gtrless 0$ as $m_c(k_c - k_i) \gtrless 0$ by noting that the numerator of expression (3.24) is positive or negative depending on whether consumption goods are exported ($m_c < 0$) or imported ($m_c > 0$) since $f_i''(k_i) < 0$. The denominator is positive or negative depending on whether consumption goods are capital or labor intensive since $A \gtrless 0$ as $k_c \lessgtr k_i$ from equation (C.4) of Appendix C, $f_i''(k_i) < 0$ and $F(m_c) - m_c F'(m_c) > 0$ by the concavity of F. These results can be combined to obtain the conclusion that θ is positive if and only if the capital intensive good is imported, that is, $m_c(k_c - k_i) > 0$ and is negative if and only if it is exported, that is, $m_c(k_c - k_i) < 0$.

Using equation (3.23) we find that under free trade, maximum sustainable consumption obtains when[1]

$$(3.25) \qquad f_i'(k_i) + \theta = \delta.$$

Letting k_G be the capital stock per worker implied by the condition $f_i'(k_i) = \delta$ and k_M be that which maximizes consumption per worker under free trade, then

$$k_M \gtrless k_G \quad \text{as} \quad m_c(k_c - k_i) \gtrless 0$$

in the neighborhood of k_M. This result follows since under free trade, $f_i'(k_i) \lessgtr \delta$ at the consumption maximizing point depending on whether $\theta \gtrless 0$ by equation (3.25), $\theta \gtrless 0$ as $m_c(k_c - k_i) \gtrless 0$ by equation (3.24) and $f_i'(k_i)$ declines as k increases. Therefore a free trading economy facing variable terms of trade maximizes steady state consumption at a larger or smaller capital stock than that dictated by the closed economy golden rule depending on whether importables are capital or labor intensive.

This result is explained as follows. Steady state consumption reaches a maximum when an additional unit of capital adds just enough product to cover its own depreciation--hence, the familiar golden rule formula. But in the free trading economy described, an additional unit of capital also depresses the relative price of the capital intensive commodity yielding a terms of trade gain if that commodity is imported and loss if it is exported. The θ term represents this terms of trade effect and is positive for terms of trade gains and negative for terms of trade losses. The maximum steady state level of consumption then occurs when the marginal

---

[1]The second order conditions require that $f_i''(k_i) + \partial\theta/\partial k_i < 0$ which is clearly a difficult proposition to prove by the definition of θ. Therefore it is assumed that the second order conditions obtain and the maximum is regular.

product of an additional unit of capital plus income changes caused by its effect on the terms of trade equal the depreciation rate, hence expression (3.25).

This and two further points are illustrated in Figure 10 where G and M are the points at which steady state consumption is maximized under autarky and free trade respectively. In panel a is illustrated the case where the capital intensive commodity is exported in the relevant portion of the I_{rT} curve while in panel b the labor intensive commodity is exported. The point at which $f_i'(k_i) = \delta$ is denoted G_T in both cases. Since the inter-temporally optimizing consumer sets $f_i'(k_i) = \rho + \delta$, it is possible for his "optimum" steady state to lie in the negatively sloped segment of I_{rT} above point M (such as point A) and clearly violate the Koopmans optimality criterion. This occurs if $f_i'(k_i) = \rho + \delta < \delta - \theta$. If $\theta < 0$ then it is possible for $-\theta > \rho > 0$ which results in a point such as A since the steady state capital stock chosen by the consumer is larger than that implied by $f_i'(k_i) + \theta = \delta$. This result occurs because price taking consumers and producers neglect the terms of trade consequences of their actions in formulating their optimizing plans. When the capital intensive commodity is exported ($\theta < 0$) the capital stock they choose is too large because they disregard the terms of trade losses resulting from increasing the capital stock. Similarly, if the capital intensive commodity is imported, the capital stock they choose is too small because the terms of trade gains in choosing a larger stock of capital are disregarded.

An interesting implication of the above analysis is that a tax on income from capital can improve welfare in economy exporting the capital intensive commodity under free trade since it would induce the consumer to

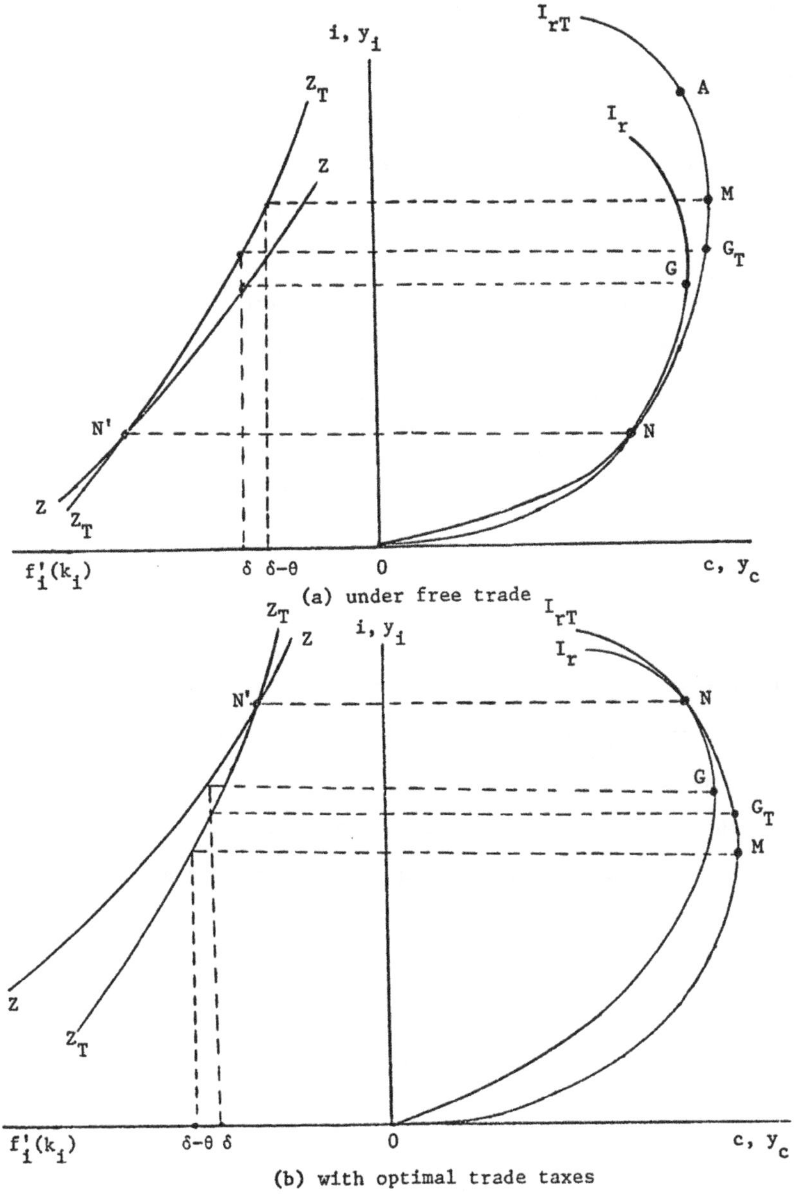

Fig. 10.--Golden rule points with trade

decumulate to a smaller equilibrium capital stock thus improving the terms of trade.

If an income tax allowing true economic depreciation were imposed, the steady state condition on q would be[1]

$$f_i'(k_i) = \rho(1 - t_y)^{-1} + \delta \tag{3.18'}$$

where t_y is an income tax on net of depreciation earnings of capital. The consumer can enjoy a maximum steady state level of consumption when $ty = (\rho + \theta)/\theta$ which is positive when $-\theta > \rho > 0$. He will be optimizing (given free trade) on an optimal path which converges to a steady state point implied by the condition $f_i'(k_i) + \theta = \rho + \delta$ which occurs when $t_y = \theta/(\theta - \rho) > 0$. This steady state will lie in the positively sloped segment of I_{rT} with a smaller capital stock than that at which steady state consumption is maximized since by substituting this value of t_y in (3.18') we get $f_i'(k_i) = \rho + \delta - \theta > \delta - \theta$, where the latter is the condition for maximum steady state consumption.

In any event, such income taxes would be second best policies because an optimal trade tax policy leads to a first best optimum. As demonstrated in a later section of this chapter, the optimal trade tax for this economy is

$$t^* = \varepsilon_F^{-1} - 1 \quad \text{where} \quad \varepsilon_F = F'(m_c)m_c/F(m_c) > 0$$

so ε_F is the elasticity of the foreign offer curve and t^* is determined to be the same as in the static economy. This optimum trade tax determines

---

[1]The relevant Hamiltonian for the case of the income tax t_y is $H = u(c) + q[(r-\delta)\ k(1-t_y) + w + \gamma - p\ c]$.

another investment requirements curve shown as I_r^* in Figure 11 which must lie to the right of all possible investment requirement curves except at N. It is derived in the same way as the free trade investment requirements curve except that the optimal trade tax Baldwin envelope curve represents consumption and investment opportunities at each level of k. The derivation of a single point on I_r^* is shown in Figure 11 where B*B* is the optimal trade tax Baldwin envelope curve which lies to the right of all other Baldwin curves except at a point of tangency.

The slope of the optimal trade tax investment requirements curve is derived in Appendix C and shown by equation (C.19) to be the same equation as the slope of the autarky investment requirements curve I_r as given by equation (3.19). It should be understood that at each value of k the values of p and $f_i'(k_i)$ differ in each case however.[1] The main point which can be established is that the point of maximum consumption on I_r^* is found by the golden rule $f_i'(k_i) = \delta$ and shown as G* in Figure 11. This point is a golden "golden rule" since steady state consumption is not only maximized over all value of k but also over all values of t. Similarly, the modified golden rule point where $f_i'(k_i) = \rho + \delta$ can be shown to be the global optimum in terms of the objective functional, as will be shown in a following section.

The Effects of Variations in Trade Taxes on Steady State Values

The steady state at a given value of the trade tax t is found by solving equations (3.9), (3.10), (3.12), (3.14) and (3.16') to (3.18). The

---

[1]Along I_r^* domestic production is more concentrated towards the good which the economy is exporting, therefore as compared to the autarky curve I_r at each value of k, p and $f_i'(k_i)$ will be higher or lower depending on which good is exported and its factor intensity.

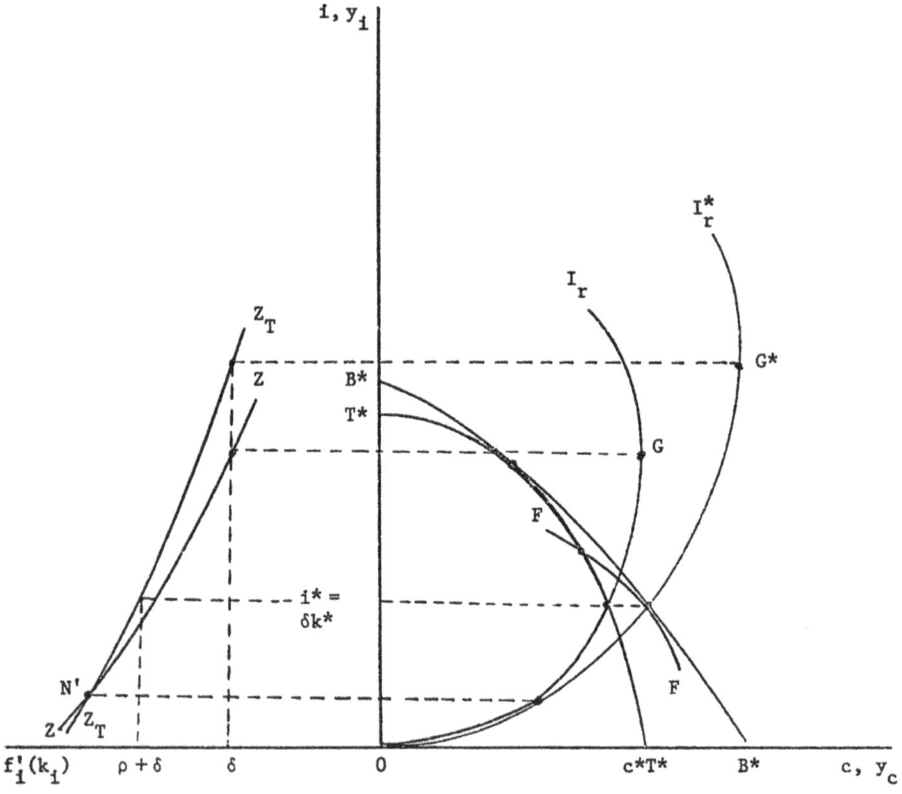

Fig. 11.--The effects of the optimal trade tax on the I_r and ZZ loci

effects of variations in t on steady state values of c and k can be analyzed by totally differentiating and manipulating these equations. The algebraic manipulations are relegated to Appendix C where the change in the optimal capital stock k* with respect to a change in t is found to be

$$(3.26) \qquad \frac{dk^*}{dt} = \frac{F'(m_c)\; p\, m_c^2\, (k_c - k_i)}{(F - m_c F')(w + \rho k_i + \delta\, k_c)}$$

from equation (C.24') of Appendix C. Since $F' < 0$ and $F - m_c F' > 0$ by the concavity of F, it is easily established that $dk^*/dt \gtrless 0$ as $k_c \lesseqgtr k_i$. If investment goods are imported, an increase in trade taxes occurs when $dt > 0$ therefore k* increases or decreases depending on whether consumption goods are labor or capital intensive. If consumption goods are imported, an increase in trade taxes occurs when $dt < 0$ and k* increases or decreases depending on whether consumption goods are capital or labor intensive. These results are combined to yield the following proposition.

Proposition 2. An increase in trade taxes increases or decreases the optimal steady state capital stock depending on whether the importable is capital or labor intensive.

The reasoning behind this proposition is that an increase in trade taxes shifts production towards the importable raising its relative price and the relative price of the factor intensive in its production at the existing value of k. But the steady state condition on q [equation (3.18)] fixes the marginal product of capital and the relative price of the commodities. Hence the factor endowment must increase relatively in terms of the factor intensive in the importable so k* rises or falls depending on whether the importable is capital or labor intensive. This result can be recognized as an inversion of the familiar Rybczynski relation.

The effects on steady state consumption are not so clear cut. Equation

(C.25''') of Appendix C gives the change in optimal steady state consumption c* resulting from a change in t as

$$(3.27) \qquad \frac{dc*}{dt} = \frac{p\, m_c^2}{F-m_c F'} \left[\frac{f_c p(1 - \varepsilon F(1+t)) - \rho(k_c - k_i)}{w + \rho k_i + \delta k_c} \right]$$

where $\varepsilon_F = F'(m_c)m_c/F(m_c) > 0$ is the elasticity of the foreign offer curve. In the next section it is demonstrated that the optimal trade tax is $t* = \varepsilon_F^{-1} - 1$, therefore if the trade tax is initially set at t*, the first term of the numerator in the large brackets in expression (3.27) is zero, hence

$$(3.27') \qquad \frac{dc*}{dt*} = \frac{-p\, m_c^2}{F-m_c F'} \left[\frac{\rho(k_c - k_i)}{w + \rho k_i + \delta k_c} \right] \gtrless 0 \quad \text{as} \quad k_c \lessgtr k_i .$$

Recalling that dt* > 0 and dt* < 0 are increases in the optimal trade tax depending on whether investment goods or consumption goods are imported respectively, the following proposition is derived from (3.27').

Proposition 3. An increase in trade taxes from the optimal level will increase or decrease the optimal steady state level of consumption depending on whether the importable is capital or labor intensive.

If the importable is capital intensive, an increase in trade taxes raises the return to capital in terms of either good at the initial k inducing the consumer to forego the now relatively more expensive present consumption in order to enjoy a higher steady state consumption in the future. Similarly, if the importable is labor intensive, the increase in trade taxes lowers the return to capital inducing the consumer to consume more now by decumulating his capital stock and having a smaller steady state consumption in the future. These results are unambiguous because small increments in the trade tax around the optimal value t* have no effects on the consumption and investment opportunities facing the consumer, that is, the position of the investment requirements curve is unchanged by such variations in the trade tax.

However, if $t \neq t^*$ then there is ambiguity as to the effect of changes in trade taxes on the steady state level of consumption in some cases because changes in non-optimal trade taxes shift the investment requirements curve. A change in trade taxes towards the optimal value t* expands the investment and consumption opportunities open to the economy while a change in trade taxes away from the optimal value diminishes them. By inspection of equation (3.27) we find that dc*/dt is ambiguous of sign, even when the factor intensities of the commodities are specified, when $\varepsilon_F(1 + t) < 1$ (that is, $t < t^*$) and $k_c > k_i$, and when $\varepsilon_F(1 + t) > 1$ (that is, $t > t^*$) and $k_c < k_i$. Both cases correspond to situations where the existing trade tax is greater than the optimal value and the importable is capital intensive, or less than the optimal value and the importable is labor intensive. In the first case, an increase in the trade tax would still induce the consumer to forego present consumption and accumulate a larger capital stock, but the steady state level of consumption may be smaller because the increase in trade taxes (away from the optimal level) reduces the steady state level of consumption possible at any value of k, hence a smaller or larger level of consumption is consistent with the larger capital stock induced by the increased trade taxes. In the second case, the consumer is induced to hold a smaller steady state capital stock but the increase in the trade tax (towards the optimal value) increases the level of steady state consumption possible at any value of k. Again the two effects work in opposite directions and the effect on the level of consumption is ambiguous.

Finally, it can be demonstrated that the sign of (3.27) is unambiguous (when factor intensities are specified) if the trade tax is greater than the optimum value and the importable is labor intensive or if the trade tax is less than the optimum value and the importable is capital intensive. In these cases, the inter-temporal effect on the size of the capital stock and the effect on the consumption and investment opportunities available at each value of k work in the same direction. An increase in trade taxes reduces the level of steady state consumption in the first case and increases it in the second case.

The Optimum Trade Tax in an Inter-temporally Optimizing Economy

Since the foreign offer curve assumed in the preceding analysis is not infinitely elastic, free trade is a non-optimal policy from the viewpoint of the domestic economy. It can now be demonstrated that, assuming no retaliation, the optimal trade tax is the same as in the conventional fixed capital stock case. This is not surprising since the source of the non-optimality is the same in both cases, that is, under free trade the marginal rate of transformation between exportables and importables in domestic production does not equal the marginal rate of transformation between the two goods made possible by trade, viz., the slope of the foreign offer curve.

To find the optimum trade tax we form the Hamiltonian[1]

$$(3.28)\qquad H = u(y_c + m_c) + q[(r-\delta)k + w - py_c - \pi m_c]$$

where $m_c = c - y_c$ and $\pi = p_c^w/p_i^w = p(1 + t)$ is the world price of consumption

---

[1]Since profits $= y_1 + py_c - rk - w = 0$ by competition, and adding $i - y_i$ and πm_c leaves this equality unchanged by equations (3.14) and (3.15), we can use equation (3.3) and solve for $\dot{k}$ to obtain equation (3.28) as $H = u(c) + q\,\dot{k}$.

goods. Applying the maximum principle independently to control variables p and π we can determine the optimum trade tax from $p^*(1+t^*) = \pi^*$ where π^* and p^* are the optimum values of the control variables. The steps are as follows.

$$(3.29) \qquad \frac{\partial H}{\partial p} = u'(\cdot)\,\frac{\partial y_c}{\partial p} + q\left[\frac{\partial(rk + w)}{\partial p} - y_c - p\,\frac{\partial y_c}{\partial p}\right] = 0$$

$$\text{or} \qquad u'(\cdot) - q\,p = 0$$

since $\partial(rk + w)/\partial p = y_c$.[1] Also

$$(3.30) \qquad \frac{\partial H}{\partial \pi} = u'(\cdot)\,\frac{\partial m_c}{\partial \pi} - q[\pi\,\frac{\partial m_c}{\partial \pi} + m_c] = 0$$

and substituting (3.29) into (3.30) to get

$$(3.31) \qquad \frac{\partial m_c}{\partial \pi}\,(p - \pi) - m_c = 0.$$

Differentiating equation (3.15) to get

$$(3.32) \qquad \frac{\partial m_c}{\partial \pi} = \frac{m_c^2}{F(m_c) - m_c F'(m_c)}$$

substituting into (3.31) and using $p(1 + t) = \pi$ to obtain

$$(3.33) \qquad 1 + t^* = 1/\varepsilon_F$$

where $\varepsilon_F = F'(m_c)m_c/F(m_c) > 0$ is the elasticity of the foreign offer curve. This is the same expression as used in obtaining the optimal trade tax in a static economy.[2]

---

[1]This is easily obtained by using $\partial r/\partial p = f_c/(k_c - k_i)$ and $\partial w/\partial p = -k_i f_c/(k_c - k_i)$ by the so-called reciprocity relation and using equation (3.9a).

[2]Noting that my $\varepsilon_F = 1/\varepsilon_{frd}$ of Johnson's notation (because I have reversed the axes of Johnson), equation (3.33) can be seen to be identical to

Fixed Terms of Trade and Intertemporal Optimization

In the preceding sections, the domestic country was assumed to face variable terms of trade. This assumption avoided certain problems of specialization or indeterminacy of domestic production which must arise if the inter-temporally optimizing economy faces a fixed world price ratio π_o. In this case, the steady state condition on q [equation (3.18)] fixes the domestic price ratio in the steady state (call it p*) as before but now the world price ratio cannot adjust to it. Therefore, under free trade specialization in domestic production must occur if $p^* \neq \pi_o$ while indeterminacy of the production point will occur in the unlikely case where $p^* = \pi_o$.

The first step is to derive the investment requirements curve for a free trading economy facing fixed terms of trade π_o. The model can now be completed with a single equation

$$(3.15') \qquad i - y_i + \pi_o(c - y_c) = 0$$

indicating that trade is balanced at the fixed world price ratio. Substituting into equation (3.8) and recalling that R = 0 by competition, we get

$$(3.34) \qquad i + \pi_o c - rk - w = 0$$

when production is non-specialized so $p = \pi_o$. Substituting equations (3.11) and (3.17) we get the straight line

$$(3.35) \qquad i = \frac{\pi_o \delta}{f'_{io} - \delta} + \lambda$$

Johnson's equation (2) in H. G. Johnson, International Trade and Economic Growth (Cambridge: Harvard University Press, 1967), pp. 56-59.

where $\lambda = -\delta w_o/(f'_{io} - \delta)$ is a constant and w_o and $f'_{io}(k_{io})$ are fixed by the condition that $p = \pi_o$. The expression in (3.35) is that of the Johnson PQ curve[1] and is shown as the linear segment of I_{rT} in Figure 12. It represents that segment of the free trade investment requirements curve for which production is unspecialized and its slope is equal to

$$(3.36) \qquad \left.\frac{di}{dc}\right|_{PQ} = \frac{\delta\pi_o}{f'_{io}(k_i) - \delta} \gtrless 0 \quad \text{as} \quad f'_{io}(k_i) \gtrless \delta.$$

Note that PQ is tangent to I_r, the autarky investment requirements curve, at point N where $y_i = \delta\, k$ and $p = \pi_o$.

The other segments of the free trade investment requirements curve correspond to points of specialized production in the domestic economy. In segment OP the economy produces only labor intensive goods and imports capital intensive goods, so $p \gtrless \pi_o$ depending on whether consumption goods are capital or labor intensive. In segment QGI_{rT} the economy produces only capital intensive goods and imports labor intensive goods with $p \gtrless \pi_o$ depending on whether consumption goods are labor or capital intensive.

The geometric derivation of points P and Q is shown in Figure 12 where RR' is a Rybczynski line (drawn without loss of generality for the case of capital intensive consumption goods) representing the non-specialized production points in the economy as k is varied and $p = \pi_o$. At a low k the economy just specializes in investment goods at point R while at a high k the economy just specializes in producing consumption goods at point R'. Between R and R', the economy is non-specialized in production and through

---

[1]Johnson, "Trade and Growth: A Geometrical Exposition," pp. 83-101. In this article, Johnson extends the PQ curve to the horizontal axis, but specialization will occur before such a point as described in the text.

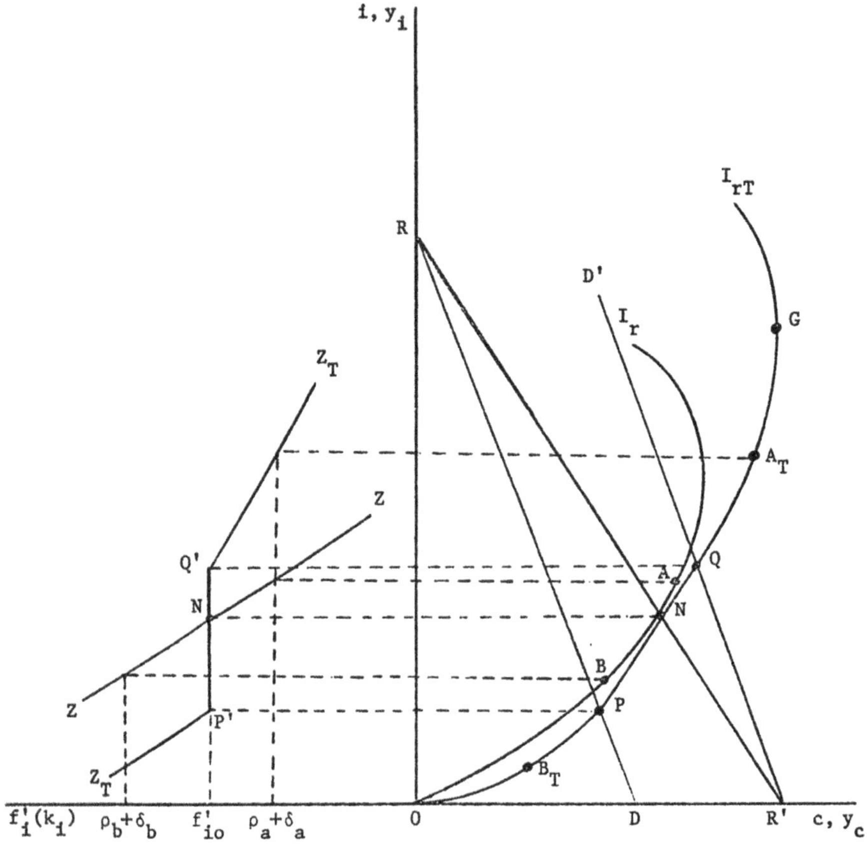

Fig. 12.--Fixed terms of trade and the steady state

any point on RR' we can draw a price line with slope $-\pi_o$ which represents the consumption and investment points open to the free trading economy producing at that point. Setting $i = \delta k$ yields the PQ segment of the I_{rT} curve as production moves from R to R'. In segment PN, the labor intensive good (which is the investment good in the illustrated example) is exported while in segment NQ the capital intensive good is exported. Extending RD and R'D' with slope $-\pi_o$ we can find points P and Q respectively. If k is smaller than that at R, the economy produces only the labor intensive commodity whose relative price declines as k contracts. This yields the OP segment of the I_{rT} curve. If k is greater than that corresponding to point R', the economy produces only capital intensive goods whose price declines as k increases, this yielding the QGI_{rT} segment of the curve. Note that I_{rT} lies to the right of I_r except at N reflecting the expanded consumption and investment opportunities resulting from trade.

The behavior of the marginal product of capital $f_i'(k_i)$ along I_{rT} is described by the Z_TZ_T line in panel b of Figure 12. The vertical segment P'Q' of Z_TZ_T corresponds to the linear PQ segment of I_{rT} along which the domestic price is fixed at π_o and the marginal product of capital fixed at $f_{io}'(k_i)$. Z_TZ_T bears the same general relationship to ZZ as in the variable terms of trade case illustrated in Figure 9 and for the same reasons.

If $\rho + \delta = \rho_a + \delta_a$ in Figure 12, the opening of trade causes the steady state to shift from A under autarky to A_T under free trade. The steady state capital stock and consumption per worker is increased and the economy becomes specialized in production of the capital intensive good and importing its needs of the labor intensive good. If $\rho + \delta = \rho_b + \delta_b$ then the steady state shifts from B under autarky to B_T under free trade. The steady state capital stock is reduced while steady state consumption may either rise or fall due to the expanded consumption opportunities made possible at each level of k by free trade. In the unlikely case where $\rho + \delta = f'_{io}(k_i)$, equations (3.17) and (3.18) do not determine a unique steady state since any point between P and Q on I_{rT} satisfies them. The capital stock may rise, fall or stay the same and similarly consumption when trade is opened.

Except for the indeterminate case, the effects of the opening of trade on steady state values in the fixed world price case are the same as with variable terms of trade except that the country becomes specialized in production. The opening of trade will increase the steady state capital stock, consumption per worker and cause specialization of production in the capital intensive good when the country has a comparative advantage in that good. The steady state capital stock will fall, consumption may rise or fall and the country becomes specialized in production of the labor intensive good if the country has a comparative advantage in that good.

The effects of trade taxes are rather difficult to analyze in the fixed world price case. We begin by noting that if a trade tax t is imposed and both goods are produced, then by equation (3.16)

(3.16") $$p(1 + t) = \pi_o$$

will obtain, where once again, a positive trade tax means that $t > 0$ if the investment good is imported and $t < 0$ if the consumption good is imported. The resulting investment requirements curve is shown as ORSUVG in Figure 13. This curve will be explained for the case of a capital intensive consumption good but the same reasoning applies, mutatis mutandis, if the investment good were capital intensive. Below point N, the consumption good was imported under free trade, hence a positive trade tax implies that $t < 0$. In

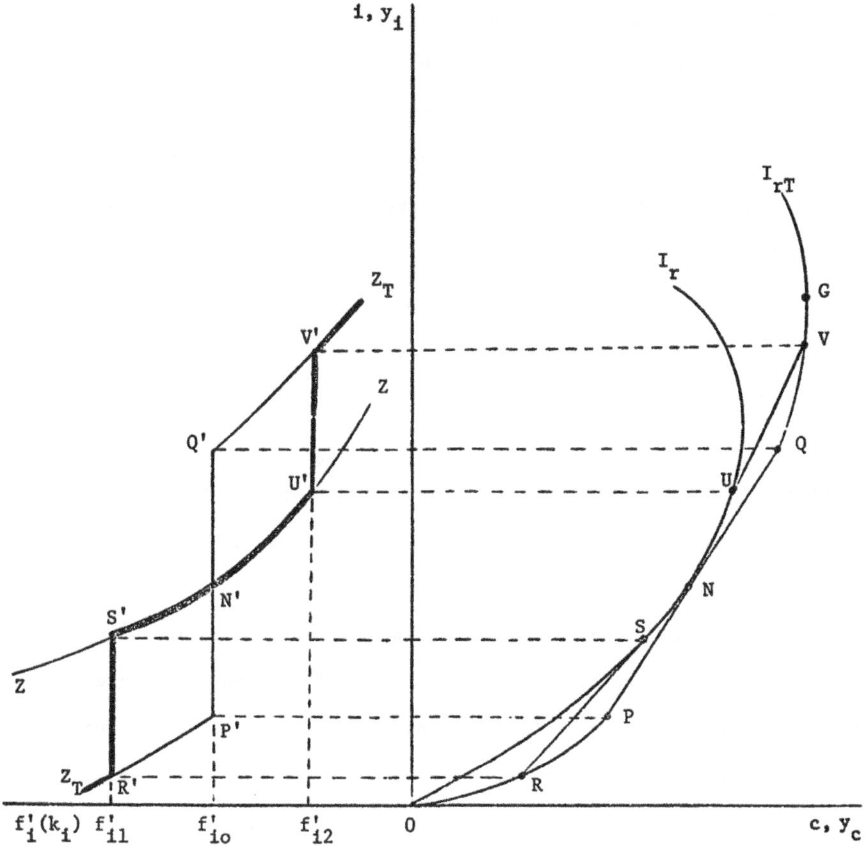

Fig. 13.--The effects of tariffs in the fixed terms of trade case

segment OR, $p(1 + t) > \pi_o$ so the economy is still specialized in producing investment goods. In fact, the trade tax has no effect in this segment since the domestic price already differed from the world price by more than the tariff. The effect of the trade tax is merely to reduce this region of production specialization. Between R and S, $p(1 + t) = \pi_o$ and production is unspecialized while the labor intensive (investment) good is exported in exchange for the capital intensive (consumption) good. Between S and N, $p(1 + t) < \pi_o$ but $p > \pi_o$ so no trade occurs. The trade tax prohibits gainful trade. Above point N, the investment good would be imported under free trade hence a positive trade tax requires that $t > 0$. In segment NU, $p(1 + t) > \pi_o$ but $p < \pi_o$ so the trade tax is prohibitive of gainful trade and no trade occurs in this segment. Between U and V, $p(1+t) = \pi_o$ and the country imports the labor intensive (investment) good and is non-specialized in production. Above V, $p(1 + t) < \pi_o$ so the country remains specialized in the production of capital intensive (consumption) goods and the trade tax has no effect except to reduce the region of specialization.

In summary, the effect of trade taxes for an inter-temporally optimizing economy facing fixed world prices is to reduce the region of specialized production, create a range of k for which no trade will occur (segment SU) and provide two linear segments of non-specialized production. Note that except for the remaining specialization regions where the trade tax has no effect because the domestic price differs from the world price by more than the tariff and point N, the investment requirements curve after trade taxes lies inside the free trade curve reflecting the inefficiency introduced by imposing the trade taxes with fixed terms of trade.

The Z_TZ_T line after taxes becomes $Z_TR'S'U'V'Z_T$ where R'S' and U'V' are vertical segments occurring at f'_{i1} and f'_{i2} and corresponding to the linear segments RS and UV of the investment requirements curve respectively. The effect of a trade tax on the steady state values can now be analyzed. If $\rho + \delta > f'_{i1}$ the trade tax has no effect and the economy remains specialized in producing the labor intensive good and importing the capital intensive good. If $f'_{i1} > \rho + \delta > f'_{i2}$, the imposition of the trade tax is prohibitive and returns the economy to its autarky state. If $\rho + \delta < f'_{i2}$, the economy remains specialized in producing the capital intensive commodity and importing the labor intensive good. In the unlikely cases of $\rho + \delta = f'_{i1}$ or f'_{i2} we have the case of an indeterminate steady state involving non-specialized production and the steady state lying anywhere between RS and UV respectively. Finally, it should be clear from the foregoing that the greater the trade tax, the smaller the "unaffected" specialization regions and the larger the region for which trade is prohibited and the economy returned to its autarky state.

Some Concluding Remarks

The basic idea in this chapter is that policies affecting a country's openness to trade, such as changing trade taxes, have two main effects in the domestic economy. The first is to change the rate of return to capital for the existing capital stock and thus induce a change in the desired capital stock. The second is to change the consumption and investment opportunities available to the economy at a given factor endowment. These two effects lie behind the results derived for this chapter on the steady state values of c and k. The impact effect on present consumption was not analyzed but it appears readily obtained. A situation which increases the desired capital stock and reduces consumption and investment opportunities must reduce present consumption and so on. Interestingly, the cases for which the effect on steady state consumption is ambiguous are unambiguous as to their effects on present consumption and vice versa.

APPENDIX A

MATHEMATICAL APPENDIX TO CHAPTER I

In this appendix, the equations presented in Chapter I are derived.

(1) Totally differentiate equations (1.1) to (1.4) to obtain

(A.1) $$z_{L1}\ DX_1 + z_{L2}\ DX_x = DL - (z_{L1}\ Da_{L1} + z_{L2}\ Da_{L2})$$

(A.2) $$z_{K1}\ DX_1 + z_{K2}\ DX_2 = DK - (z_{K1}\ Da_{K1} + z_{K2}\ Da_{K2})$$

(A.3) $$v_{L1}\ Dp_L + v_{K1}\ Dp_K = Dp + DT_S - v_{K1}\ DT_C$$

(A.4) $$v_{L2}\ Dp_L + v_{K2}\ Dp_K = 0$$

where the z_{ij}, v_{ij} are the physical and value shares. Equations (A.3) and (A.4) were obtained using

(A.5) $$v_{Li}\ Da_{Li} + v_{Ki}\ Da_{Ki} = 0 \quad \text{for } i = 1, 2.$$

Letting $\sigma_i > 0$ be the elasticity of substitution of production in X_i we get:

(A.6) $$Da_{K1} - Da_{L1} = \sigma_1(Dp_L - Dp_K - DT_C)$$

(A.7) $$Da_{K2} - Da_{L2} = \sigma_2(Dp_L - Dp_K).$$

Using (A.5) we see:

(A.8) $$Da_{i1} = (1 - v_{i1})\ \sigma_1(Dp_L - Dp_K - DT_C)$$

(A.9) $$Da_{i2} = (1 - v_{i2})\ \sigma_2(Dp_L - Dp_K)$$

for $i = L, K$. Substituting into (A.1) and (A.2), using $v_{Lj} + v_{Kj} = 1$ and fixing factor supplies (hence $DL = DK = 0$) we derive:

$$\text{(A.10)} \qquad |z|(DX_1 - DX_2) = (\delta_1\sigma_1 + \delta_2\sigma_2)(Dp_L - Dp_K) - \delta_1\sigma_1\, DT_C$$

where $\delta_i = z_{Li}v_{Ki} + z_{Ki}v_{Li} > 0$ and $|z|$ is defined by equation (1.6) of the text. Subtracting (A.4) from (A.3)

$$\text{(A.11)} \qquad |v|(Dp_L - Dp_K) = Dp + DT_S - v_{K1}\, DT_C$$

where $|v|$ is defined by equation (1.7) of the text. Substituting (A.11) into (A.10), the aggregate supply curve in differential form as given by equation (1.5) of the text is obtained as

$$\text{(A.12)} \qquad DX_1 - DX_2 = \left(\frac{\delta_1\sigma_1 + \delta_2\sigma_2}{|z|\ |v|}\right)(Dp + DT_S) - \left(\frac{v_{K2}\delta_1\sigma_1 + v_{K1}\delta_2\sigma_2}{|z|\ |v|}\right)DT_C$$

Now using the homothetic demand relation

$$\text{(A.13)} \qquad DX_1 - DX_2 = -\sigma_D\, Dp$$

where σ_D is the elasticity of substitution in consumption, we can solve (A.12) and (A.13) simultaneously to get:

$$\text{(A.14)} \qquad Dp_K - Dp_L = \frac{(v_{K1}\sigma_D|z| - \delta_1\sigma_1)DT_C - (|z|\sigma_D)DT_S}{\delta_1\sigma_1 + \delta_2\sigma_2 + |z|\ |v|\ \sigma_D}$$

which is equation (1.10) of the text. Considering only a tax on capital in sector 1, we can set $DT_S = 0$ to get

$$\text{(A.14')} \qquad Dp_K - Dp_L = \left(\frac{v_{K1}\sigma_D|z| - \delta_1\sigma_1}{\delta_1\sigma_1 + \delta_2\sigma_2 + |z||v|\sigma_D}\right)DT_C$$

where the expression in large parentheses is the elasticity between the rental-wage ratio and the corporation income tax rate.

(2) Discrete changes in the corporation income tax.

Let $p_K/p_L = \omega$ and equation (A.14') becomes

$$D\omega = E_{fT}(T_C)DT_C \tag{A.14"}$$

where $E_{fT}(T_C) = \partial\omega/\partial T_C \cdot T_C/\omega$ is the expression in parentheses. Since the terms constituting E_{fT} depend on the value of T_C, E_{fT} is denoted as a function of T_C which is one plus the corporation income tax rate.

The effects of discrete changes in T_C on ω can be calculated on the assumption that E_{fT} or $E_{fT}\ \omega/T_C$ is a constant. Alternatively, $E_{fT}(T_C)$ can be differentiated with respect to T_C and second order approximations calculated. The algebraic details of the latter are now presented based on the assumption that all elasticities of substitution are unaffected by the tax.

Since $z_{Kj}/z_{Lj} = K_jL/KL_j$, then

$$Dz_{K1} - Dz_{L1} = DK_1 - DL_1 = -\sigma_1(1 + E_{fT})DT_C \tag{A.15}$$

$$Dz_{K2} - Dz_{L2} = DK_2 - DL_2 = -\sigma_2\ E_{fT}\ DT_C \tag{A.16}$$

while using $z_{j1} + z_{j2} = 1$ we obtain:

$$Dz_{j1} = \frac{-z_{j2}}{z_{j1}} Dz_{j2} \qquad j = L, K. \tag{A.17}$$

Recalling $Dx = dx/x$ we can substitute (A.17) into (A.15) and (A.16) to get

$$dz_{K1} = \frac{-z_{K1}z_{K2}(z_{L2}E_{fT}\sigma_2 + z_{L1}\sigma_1(1 + E_{fT})}{|z|} DT_C \tag{A.18}$$

$$dz_{L1} = \frac{-z_{L1}z_{L2}(z_{K2}E_{fT}\sigma_2 + z_{K1}\sigma_1(1 + E_{fT})}{|z|} DT_C\ . \tag{A.19}$$

Hence

(A.20) $$d|z| = dz_{K1} - dz_{L1} = (z_{K1}z_{L1}(E_{fT}+1)\sigma_1 - z_{K2}z_{L2}E_{fT}\sigma_2)DT_C.$$

By the definition of the v_{ij} terms we find

(A.21) $$Dv_{K1} - Dv_{L1} = (1-\sigma_1)(E_{fT}+1)DT_C$$

(A.22) $$Dv_{K2} - Dv_{L2} = (1-\sigma_2)\ E_{fT}\ DT_C$$

and since $v_{Lj} + v_{Kj} = 1$ we get

(A.23) $$Dv_{Lj} = \frac{-v_{Kj}}{v_{Lj}} Dv_{Kj} \qquad j = 1,\ 2.$$

By substitution:

(A.24) $$dv_{K1} = v_{K1}v_{L1}(1-\sigma_1)(E_{fT}+1)DT_C$$

(A.25) $$dv_{K2} = v_{K2}v_{L2}(1-\sigma_2)\ E_{fT}\ DT_C$$

and

(A.26) $$d|v| = dv_{K2} - dv_{K1} = \big(v_{K2}v_{L2}(1-\sigma_2)E_{fT} - v_{K1}v_{L1}(1-\sigma_1)(1+E_{fT})\big)DT_C.$$

Substituting Harberger's values

(A.27)
$$\begin{array}{lll} v_{K1} = 1/6 & z_{L1} = 10/11 & \sigma_1 = \sigma_D = 1 \\ v_{K2} = 1/2 & z_{K1} = 1/2 & \sigma_2 = 1/2 \\ |v| = 1/3 & |z| = .4090909 & \end{array}$$

into (A.18), (A.19), (A.20), (A.24), (A.25) and (A.26) we get

$$dv_{K1} = 0 \qquad\qquad dz_{K1} = -.2131386\ DT_C$$

(A.28) $$dv_{K2} = -.073375\ DT_C \qquad\qquad dz_{L1} = -.0120706\ DT_C$$

$$d|v| = -.073375\ DT_C \qquad\qquad d|z| = +.201068\ DT_C$$

Evaluating E_{fT} using values (A.27) we find the numerator N to be -.5 and the denominator Ð (to distinguish from operator D) to be +.8522727. By the quotient rule of differentiation we see

(A.29) $$dE_{fT} = \left(\frac{1}{Ð}\right)dN - \left(\frac{N}{Ð^2}\right)dÐ$$

$$= 1.173334\ dN + .688356\ dÐ\,.$$

Using $\sigma_D = \sigma_1 = 1$, the numerator N can be reduced to $N = -z_{K1}$ by algebraic manipulation, therefore

(A.30) $$dN = -\ dz_{K1} = +.2131386\ DT_C$$

by (A.28). By using $\sigma_D = \sigma_1 = 1$ and $\sigma_2 = 1/2$, the denominator can be algebraically reduced to:

(A.31) $$Ð = \frac{1}{2}(1 + z_{L1}v_{K2} + z_{K1}v_{L2})$$

and

(A.32) $$dÐ = \frac{1}{2}(v_{K2}\ dz_{L1} + v_{L2}\ dz_{K1} + |z|dv_{K2})$$

where $dz_{j1} = -dz_{j2}$ and $dv_{Kj} = -dv_{Lj}$ were used. Using (A.28) we can evaluate

(A.32') $$dÐ = -.0713106\ DT_C$$

and by substituting (A.30) and (A.32') into (A.29) we find

(A.33) $$dE_{fT} = .201\ DT_C\ .$$

Recalling $DT_C = dT_C/T_C$ and that at the post tax point $T_C = 2$ we see

(A.33') $$\frac{dE_{fT}}{dT_C} = .1005 \approx .1\ .$$

Alternatively,

(A.34) $$\frac{D|E_{fT}|}{DT_C} = \frac{dE_{fT}}{dT_C} \cdot \frac{T_C}{|E_{fT}|} = -.3408$$

as evaluated at the post-tax point. Second order (i.e., quadratic) approximations of the effect of a discrete change in T_C on the rental-wage ratio can now be calculated. In the text, this is done under the alternate assumptions that dE_{fT}/dT_C or $D|E_{dT}|/DT_C$ are constants.

(3) General equilibrium incidence with non-identical tastes.

When households can be divided up into g groups such that within each group tastes are identical and homothetic, the commodity demand relation will be as shown in equation (1.17) of the text, repeated as (A.35) below.

(A.35) $$DX_1 - DX_2 = -\bar{\sigma}_D\ Dp + \Sigma_g^r\ m^g s_L^g\ (Dp_L - Dp_K)$$

where $\bar{\sigma}_D$, m^g and s_L^g are defined in the text. Substituting equation (A.11) we get:

(A.36) $$DX_1 - DX_2 = \left[\frac{\Sigma_g^r\ m^g s_L^g}{|v|} - \bar{\sigma}_D\right] Dp + \frac{\Sigma_g^r\ m^g s_L^g}{|v|}\ (DT_S - v_{K1}\ DT_C)\ .$$

This can be solved simultaneously with (A.12) to get

(A.37) $$(\alpha - \bar{\sigma}_D - \beta)Dp + (\alpha - \beta)DT_S + (\gamma - v_{K1}\alpha)DT_C = 0$$

where

$$\alpha = \frac{\Sigma_g^r m^g s_L^g}{|v|}, \qquad \beta = \frac{\delta_1\sigma_1 + \delta_2\sigma_2}{|v|\ |z|}$$

and

$$\gamma = \frac{v_{K2}\delta_1\sigma_1 + v_{K1}\delta_2\sigma_2}{|v|\ |z|}.$$

Then using (A.11) we get:

$$\text{(A.38)} \qquad (\bar{\sigma}_D + \beta - \alpha)|v|\ (Dp_L - Dp_K) = \bar{\sigma}_D\ DT_S + (\gamma - v_{K1}\ \bar{\sigma}_D - v_{K1}\beta)DT_C$$

which can be solved for

$$\text{(A.39)} \qquad Dp_K - Dp_L = \frac{(\bar{\sigma}_D\ v_{K1}|z| - \delta_1\sigma_1)DT_C - \bar{\sigma}_D|z|\ DT_S}{\delta_1\sigma_1 + \delta_2\sigma_2 + |z||v|\bar{\sigma}_D - |z| \cdot \Sigma_g^r\ m^g s_L^g}$$

which is equation (1.18).

In the text, Dy^g is defined as the percentage change in the factor income of group g minus the percentage change in the cost of its pre-tax commodity bundle. Then, for any two groups a and b we got:

$$\text{(A.40)} \qquad Dy^a - Dy^b = [(s_L^b - s_L^a)(Dp_K - Dp_L) + (s_1^h - s_1^a)Dp$$

where s_L^g and s_1^g are as defined in the text.

In the case in which only the sales tax is increased (that is, $DT_S < 0$ and $DT_C = 0$) we can substitute equation (A.11) into (A.40) to get

$$\text{(A.41)} \qquad Dy^a - Dy^b = [(s_L^b - s_L^a) - (s_1^b - s_1^a)|v|](Dp_K - Dp_L) - (s_1^b - s_1^a)DT_S\ .$$

Then using equation (A.14) which solves for $Dp_K - Dp_L$ in terms of DT_S, we get:

$$\text{(A.42)} \qquad Dy^a - Dy^b = \frac{[(s_1^b - s_1^a)(|z|\Sigma_g^r m^g s_L^g - \delta_1\sigma_1 - \delta_2\sigma_2) - (s_L^b - s_L^a)\bar{\sigma}_D|z|]}{\delta_1\sigma_1 + \delta_2\sigma_2 + \bar{\sigma}_D|z||v| - \Sigma_g^r\ m^g s_L^g}\ DT_S$$

which is equation (1.19) of the text. Assuming that the denominator of (A.42) remains positive, it is clear that whether $Dy^a \gtrless Dy^b$ for a given DT_S depends on the sign of the numerator. Unfortunately, the numerator is ambiguous of sign in that specification of the commodity preferences and factor shares of the groups will not generally suffice to sign the numerator. For example, if a and b are the only groups then:

$$\Sigma_g^r m^g s_L^g = m^a s_L^a + m^b s_L^b = - m^a (s_L^b - s_L^a)$$

since $\Sigma_g^r m^g = 0$. Substituting into the numerator of (A.42) and rearranging we find that for an increase in the excise tax on X_1 (i.e., $DT_S < 0$) we get

$$\text{(A.43)} \quad Dy^a - Dy^b \gtrless 0 \text{ as } (s_1^b - s_1^a)(\delta_1\sigma_1 + \delta_2\sigma_2) + |z|(s_L^b - s_L^a)\left(\bar{\sigma}_0 = m^a(s_1^b - s_1^a)\right) \gtrless 0$$

which is equation (1.20). Furthermore, $m^a(s_1^b - s_1^a) < 0$ since:

$$m^a(s_1^b - s_1^a) = m^a \left(\frac{pX_1^b}{pX_1^b + X_2^b} - \frac{pX_1^a}{pX_1^a - X_2^a} \right)$$

$$= pm^a \left(\frac{X_1^b X_2^a - X_1^a X_2^b}{(pX_1^b + X_2^b)(pX_1^a + X_2^a)} \right).$$

Using $X_i^a + X_i^b = X_i$ we can continue:

$$m^a(s_1^b - s_1^a) = pm^a \left(\frac{X_2^a X_1 - X_1^a X_2}{(pX_1^b + X_2^b)(pX_1^a + X_2^a)} \right)$$

$$= \frac{pm^a X_1 X_2}{(pX_1^b + X_2^b)(pX_1^a + X_2^a)} \left(\frac{X_2^a}{X_2} - \frac{X_1^a}{X_1} \right)$$

$$= \frac{- pX_1 X_2 (m^a)^2}{(pX_1^b + X_2^b)(pX_1^a + X_2^a)} < 0.$$

Therefore the sign of $\bar{\sigma}_D - m^a(s_1^b - s_1^a)$ is ambiguous unless $\bar{\sigma}_D > 1$ in which case it is positive since m^a and $(s_1^b - s_1^a)$ are both smaller than unity.

APPENDIX B

MATHEMATICAL APPENDIX TO CHAPTER II

In this appendix, certain propositions asserted in Chapter II are proved.

1) The general equilibrium demand curve and the integrability conditions.

The general equilibrium demand curve is obtained when the consumer

(B.1) maximizes $U(X)$ subject to

(B.2) $\Sigma_i^n (1 + t_i)X_i = I + R$

and the (linear) production constraint

(B.3) $\Sigma X_i = M$ (where M is constant)

obtains. The p_i are all unity by choice of the units of the X_i and R represents the tax proceeds redistributed as a lump sum payment. The $n+1$ first order conditions

(B.4.1) to
(B.4.n) $U_i(X) = \lambda(1 + t_i)$

(B.3) $\sum_i^n X_i = M$

are differentiated to obtain:

(B.5)
$$\begin{pmatrix} U_{11} & \cdots & U_{1n} & 1+t_1 \\ \vdots & & & \vdots \\ U_{n1} & \cdots & U_{nn} & 1+t_n \\ 1 & \cdots & 1 & 0 \end{pmatrix} \begin{pmatrix} dX_1 \\ \vdots \\ dX_n \\ d\lambda \end{pmatrix} = \begin{pmatrix} -\lambda dt_1 \\ \vdots \\ -\lambda dt_n \\ 0 \end{pmatrix}$$

or

(B.5')
$$dX = - \left(\begin{array}{c|c} U_{ij} & 1+t_i \\ \hline 1 & 0 \end{array}\right)^{-1} \lambda dt \, .$$

Hence

(B.6)
$$\frac{\partial X_i}{\partial t_j} = \frac{-\lambda D_{ij}}{D}$$

$$\frac{\partial X_j}{\partial t_i} = \frac{-\lambda D_{ji}}{D}$$

where D_{ij} is the ij^{th} cofactor and D is the determinant of the matrix in equation (B.5). Therefore the integrability conditions require that $D_{ij} = D_{ji}$. By a well known theorem on symmetric matrices, the inverse of a symmetric matrix is symmetric therefore the integrability conditions require that the matrix in (B.5) be symmetric. This will hold under two conditions:

(a) That $t_i = 0$ for all i. Then since $U_{ij} = U_{ji}$ by the integrability conditions on the utility function, $D^o_{ij} = D^o_{ji}$ where the superscript denotes the zero tax case.

(b) That $t_i = t_j = t$ for all i, j. Then

$$\frac{\partial X_i}{\partial t_j} = \frac{(1+t)D^o_{ij}}{(1+t)D^o} = \frac{D^o_{ij}}{D^o}$$

while

$$\frac{\partial X_j}{\partial t_i} = \frac{(1 + t)D^o_{ji}}{(1 + t)D^o} = \frac{D^o_{ji}}{D^o}$$

In summary, for small changes around the undistorted equilibrium, the general equilibrium demand curve will satisfy the integrability conditions. The undistorted equilibrium will obtain either because all taxes are zero or because all tax rates are equal.

2) Conditions for path independence of a Divisia welfare cost index expressed in units of a numeraire good.

Consider first the case of a linear production set where units of the commodities are set so that all net of tax prices are equal to unity. That is, units of the commodity vector $\underline{X} = (X_1, \ldots, X_n)$ are set such that

(B.7) $$\Sigma_i X_i = M$$

represents the linear transformation surface and M is a constant. Then the Divisia Index for welfare cost associated with an increment of tax vector $\underline{t} = (t_1, \ldots, t_{n-1})$ from $\underline{t}^0$ to $\underline{t}^1$ is

(B.8) $$\int_{\underline{t}^0}^{\underline{t}^1} \Sigma_i \Sigma_j t_i (\partial X_i/\partial t_j) dt_j$$

where $t_n^0 = t_n^1 = 0$ and X_n is the "numeraire" good. By the first order conditions for a constrained maximum:

(B.9) $$1 + t_i = \frac{U_i(X)}{U_n(\underline{X})} = R^{in}(\underline{X})$$

and furthermore

$$dX_i = \Sigma_j(\partial X_i/\partial t_j) dt_j .$$

Hence under certain continuity conditions on utility function U and normality assumptions regarding income elasticities, there exists a one-to-one transformation with non-vanishing Jacobian so that equation (B.8) can be transformed to:

$$\text{(B.10)} \qquad \int_{\underline{X}^2}^{\underline{X}^1} \Sigma_i [R^{in}(\underline{X}) - 1] \, dX_i$$

which now expresses "welfare cost" in units of X_n, the numeraire good, and where $\underline{X}^0$ and $\underline{X}^1$ denote the equilibrium commodity vectors corresponding to the pre and post increment tax vectors respectively.

Equation (B.10) is a line integral where $\{R^{1n} - 1, R^{2n} - 1, . . .\}$ is a vector field F defined in some region D of R^n.

Now line integral $\int_\gamma F \cdot d\underline{X}$ is said to be independent of the path of integration when

$$\text{(B.11)} \qquad \int_{\delta(\underline{X}^0, \underline{X}^1)} F(\underline{X}) \cdot d\underline{X} = \int_{\gamma(\underline{X}^0, \underline{X}^1)} F(\underline{X}) \cdot d\underline{X}$$

where $\delta(\underline{X}^0, \underline{X}^1)$ and $\gamma(\underline{X}^0, \underline{X}^1)$ are any two piecewise smooth curves in D, both having initial point $\underline{X}^0$ and terminal point $\underline{X}^1$.

By Stokes-Greens theorem, the line integral will be independent of path of integration if

$$\text{(B.12)} \qquad \partial F_i/\partial X_j = \partial F_j/\partial X_i \quad \text{for all } i, j.$$

That is, the Jacobian matrix of F is symmetric (or curl F = 0 when i, j = 1 or 2). This obtains if $R^n \overset{F}{\rightarrow} R^n$ is a continuously differentiable gradient field since then there exists a function U such that grad U = F and (B.12) follows from the integrability condition on U. The above can be used to demonstrate that any line integral along an indifference surface of U is path independent.

However, the Divisia index calculated on market data is in fact a line integral which is integrated along a transformation surface. It will now be demonstrated that a necessary and sufficient condition for the path independence of this line integral when the transformation surface is a hyperplane is that the marginal utility of income be constant for all possible paths along that transformation hyperplane.

Equation (B.12) requires that:

(B.12') $$\partial R^{in}/\partial X_j = \partial R^{jn}/\partial X_i \quad \text{for all } i, j.$$

Using the definition of $R^{in}(\underline{X})$ in equation (B.9) and constraining all paths to the transformation surface defined by equation (B.7), we see that:

(B.13) $$\frac{\partial R^{in}}{\partial X_j} = \frac{U_n(U_{ij} - U_{in}) - U_i(U_{nj} - U_{nn})}{U_n^2}$$

(B.14) $$\frac{\partial R^{jn}}{\partial X_i} = \frac{U_n(U_{ji} - U_{jn}) - U_j(U_{ni} - U_{nn})}{U_n^2} .$$

Equation (B.12') obtains if the numerators in (B.13) and (B.14) are equal so dividing (B.13) and (B.14) by U_n, using $U_{ij} = U_{ji}$ and $1 + t_1 = U_i/U_n$ we can see after rearranging that (B.12') obtains if:

(B.15) $$t_i \, (U_{nj}/U_{nn}) - t_j \, (U_{ni}/U_{nn}) = t_i - t_j .$$

But (B.15) must hold for all possible values of t_i and t_j, hence $U_{nj}/U_{nn} = U_{ni}/U_{nn} = 1$, which, in turn, must hold for all i and j. Therefore, the Divisia line integral is independent of the path of integration if:

(B.16) $$U_{n1} = U_{n2} = \ldots U_{ni} = \ldots U_{nn}\,.$$

It will now be shown that for paths constrained to the transformation surface, (B.16) implies and is implied by a constant marginal utility of income.

By the first order conditions $U_n(\underline{X}) = \lambda$ where λ is the marginal utility of income (recalling X_n is untaxed and is the numeraire good). Hence $\Sigma_i\, U_{ni}\, dX_i = d\lambda$ and providing that $U_{nn} \neq 0$ and since $\Sigma_i\, dX_i = 0$ by (B.7) we see that $U_{nn} \cdot \Sigma_i\, dX_i = d\lambda = 0$ so that λ must be a constant for all variations along the transformation plane if (B.16) obtains.

Conversely it can be demonstrated that λ being a constant for all paths on the transformation plane must imply (B.16) and therefore pth independency of the Divisia line integral. Let $\Sigma_i\, U_{ni}\, dX_i = 0$ for some variation vector $d\underline{X}$ along the transformation surface, and let $U_{nk} \neq U_{n\ell}$. Then it is possible to choose some variation vector $d\underline{X}'$ satisfying $\Sigma_i\, dX_i' = 0$ so that $\Sigma_i\, U_{ni}\, dX_i' \neq 0$. For example, let $d\underline{X}'$ have all elements in common with $d\underline{X}$ except that $dX_k' = dX_\ell$ and $dX_\ell' = dX_k$. Clearly $d\underline{X}'$ is a movement along the transformation plane but $\Sigma_i\, U_{ni}\, dX_i'$ cannot now be equal to zero if $U_{nk} \neq U_{n\ell}$. Hence, λ being a constant for all variations along the transformation surface is sufficient for path independence of the Divisia line integral.

The above proof can be extended to a non-linear convex production surface by replacing (B.7) with (B.7') below.

(B.7') $$\pi(X_1, \ldots, X_n) = 0.$$

Then the first order conditions require that

(B.9') $$(1 + t_i)\, Z^{in}(\underline{X}) = R^{in}(\underline{X})$$

where $Z^{in}(\underline{X}) = \pi_i(\underline{X})/\pi_n(\underline{X})$. Therefore the Divisia welfare cost index in equation (B.10) becomes

(B.10') $$\int_{\underline{X}^2}^{\underline{X}^1} \Sigma_i^n\, [R^{in}(\underline{X}) - Z^{in}(\underline{X})]dX_i$$

and the preceding proof will hold in its entirety if

$$\frac{\partial Z^{in}(\underline{X})}{\partial X_j} = \frac{\partial Z^{jn}}{\partial X_i} \quad \text{for all } i \text{ and } j.$$

This condition holds by the integrability conditions on the production surface since all paths between $\underline{X}^2$ and $\underline{X}^1$ are constrained to that surface.

Formally, we can solve (B.7') for

$$X_n = T(X_1, \ldots X_{n-1}) = T(\underline{X}')$$

where $\underline{X}'$ is the vector $\underline{X}$ minus the nth element and

$$T_i = -Z^{in} = \frac{-\pi_i}{\pi_n}.$$

Writing

$$Z^{in}(\underline{X}') = \frac{\pi_i(\underline{X}', T(\underline{X}'))}{\pi_n(\underline{X}', T(\underline{X}'))}$$

we see that:

$$\frac{\partial Z^{in}}{\partial X_j} = \frac{\pi_n\pi_{ij} - \pi_{in}\pi_j - \pi_i\pi_{nj} + \pi_i\pi_j\pi_{nn}(\pi_n)^{-1}}{\pi_n^2}$$

$$\frac{\partial Z^{jn}}{\partial X_i} = \frac{\pi_n\pi_{ji} - \pi_{jn}\pi_i - \pi_j\pi_{ni} + \pi_i\pi_j\pi_{nn}(\pi_n)^{-1}}{\pi_n^2}$$

Since $\pi_{ij} = \pi_{ji}$, $\frac{\partial Z^{in}}{\partial X_j} = \frac{\partial Z^{jn}}{\partial X_i}$ so the line integral in (B.10') will be path independent whenever (B.10) is.

APPENDIX C

MATHEMATICAL APPENDIX TO CHAPTER III

<u>The Closed Economy</u>

Totally differentiate equations (3.9a), (3.9b) and (3.12) to get:

(C.1) $$dy_c = \frac{f_c}{k_c-k_i}\,dk + \frac{f_c(k-k_c)}{(k_c-k_i)^2}\,dk_i + \frac{f_c'f_i(k_i-k)}{f_i'(k_c-k_i)}\,dk_c$$

(C.2) $$dy_i = \frac{-f_i}{k_c-k_i}\,dk + \frac{f_cf_i(k_c-k)}{f_c'(k_c-k_i)^2}\,dk_i + \frac{f_i(k_c-k_i)}{(k_c-k_i)^2}\,dk_c$$

(C.3) $$dk_c = \frac{(f_c')^2 f_i f_i''}{(f_i')^2 f_c f_c''}\,dk_i\,.$$

Substituting (C.3) into (C.1) and (C.2)

(C.1') $$dy_c = \frac{f_c}{k_c-k_i}\,dk + A\cdot dk_i$$

(C.2') $$dy_i = \frac{-f_i}{k_c-k_i}\,dk - A\cdot p\cdot dk_i$$

where

(C.4) $$A = \frac{(f_c')^3 f_i^2 f_i''(k_i-k) + (f_i')^3 f_c^2 f_c''(k-k_c)}{(f_i')^2 f_c' f_c f_c''(k_c-k_i)^2} \gtrless 0 \text{ as } k_c \lessgtr k_i\,.$$

Also differentiate equation (3.10) and use (C.3) to get

(C.5) $$dp = \frac{f_i''(k_c-k_i)}{f_c}\,dk_i\,.$$

The I_r curve is found by solving equations (3.9), (3.12) and (3.17) simultaneously which gives

$$(C.6) \qquad (y_i, y_c) = \phi(k)$$

where the I_r curve of Figure 8 is obtained by plotting (y_i, y_c) as k is varied between 0 and ∞. The slope of I_r is found by multiplying (C.1') by p, adding to (C.2') and using equations (3.10) and (3.12) to obtain:

$$(C.7) \qquad dy_i + pdy_c = f_i'(k_i)dk.$$

Using $dy_i = \delta \cdot dk$ we get

$$(C.8) \qquad \left.\frac{dy_i}{dy_c}\right|_{I_r} = \left.\frac{di}{dc}\right|_{I_r} = \frac{p \cdot \delta}{f_i'(k_i) - \delta} \gtrless 0 \text{ as } f_i'(k_i) \gtrless \delta.$$

The slope of the ZZ line is found by using $d(f_i') = f_i''(k_i)dk_i$ where $f_i''(k_i) < 0$, and substituting with $dy_i = \delta \cdot dk$ into (C.2') to get:

$$(C.9) \qquad dy_i\left(\frac{f_i + \delta(k_c - k_i)}{\delta(k_c - k_i)}\right) = \left(\frac{-A \cdot p}{f_i''(k_i)}\right) d(f_i').$$

Adding and subtracting $f_i'(k_i) \cdot k_i$ to the numerator of the left hand side term, using equation (3.11) and rearranging we get the slope of ZZ as:

$$(C.10) \qquad \left.\frac{dy_i}{d(f_i')}\right|_{I_r} = \frac{-\delta \cdot p \cdot A(k_c - k_i)}{f_i''(w + \delta k_c + f_i' - \delta)k_i)} .$$

Note that this term is negative when $f_i' > \delta$ since $A(k_c - k_i) < 0$ by equation (C.4). Also, using equation (C.5) we can obtain

$$(C.11) \qquad \left.\frac{dp}{dy_i}\right|_{I_r} = \frac{-f_i''(w + \delta k_c + (f_i' - \delta)k_i)}{p \cdot f_c \cdot \delta \cdot A} \gtrless 0 \text{ as } k_c \lessgtr k_i.$$

Therefore p rises or falls as you move out along the I_r curve depending on whether consumption goods are labor or capital intensive.

Free Trade and Variable Terms of Trade

Differentiate (3.14) and (3.16') to get

(C.12) $$di - dy_i = F'(m_c)(dc - dy_c)$$

(C.13) $$dp = \frac{F(m_c) - F'(m_c)m_c}{m_c^2}(dc - dy_c)$$

where $m_c = c - y_c$ and $F(m_c) - F'(m_c)m_c > 0$ by the concavity of $F(m_c)$.

Substituting $di = \delta \cdot dk$ into (C.7) to get

(C.7') $$dy_i + p \cdot dy_c = \frac{f_i'(k_i)}{\delta} di$$

and summing (C.7') with (C.12), using $p + F'(m_c) = -\frac{F(m_c) - F'(m_c)m_c}{m_c}$ from equation (3.16'), and rearranging to get

(C.14) $$dy_c = \frac{-(f_i' - \delta)m_c}{\delta(F - m_c \cdot F')} di - \frac{F'(m_c)m_c}{F - m_c \cdot F'} dc .$$

Now substituting $di = \delta \cdot dk$ and equation (C.5) into equation (C.1') to obtain:

(C.15) $$dy_c = \frac{(f_i'' f_c)di + \left[\frac{\delta \cdot A \cdot f_c(F - m_c \cdot F')}{m_c^2}\right]dc}{\delta \cdot f_i''(k_c - k_i) + \frac{\delta \cdot A \cdot f_c(F - m_c \cdot F')}{m_c^2}} .$$

Substituting (C.15) into (C.14) and rearranging we obtain the slope of the free trade investment requirements curve as:

(C.16) $$\left.\frac{di}{dc}\right|_{I_{rT}} = \frac{-\beta\delta}{f_i'(k_i) + \theta - \delta}$$

where

$$(C.17) \qquad -\beta = \frac{p - \dfrac{F'(m_c)m_c^2 f_i''(k_c - k_i)}{Af_c(F - m_c \cdot F')}}{1 + \dfrac{m_c^2 f_i''(k_c - k_i)}{Af_c(F - m_c \cdot F')}} > 0$$

since $f_i''(k_c - k_i)A^{-1} > 0$, $F - m_c \cdot F' > 0$ and $F' < 0$. And

$$(C.18) \qquad \theta = \frac{m_c f_c f_i''(k_i)}{A \cdot f_c + \dfrac{f_i''(k_i)m_c^2(k_c - k_i)}{F(m_c) - m_c \cdot F(m_c)}}$$

where $\theta \gtrless 0$ as $m_c(k_c - k_i) \gtrless 0$. That is θ is positive or negative depending on whether the capital or labor intensive good is imported.

The slope of the investment requirements curve I_r^* when the optimal trade tax $t^* = F(m_c)/F'(m_c)m_c - 1$ is imposed is found by noting that $p(1 + t^*) = -F(m_c)/m_c$ from equation (3.16') implies that $p = -F'(m_c)$. Therefore adding (C.7) to (C.12) and using $di = \delta\, dk$ yields

$$(C.19) \qquad \left.\frac{di}{dc}\right|_{I_r^*} = \frac{p \cdot \delta}{f_i'(k_i) - \delta} \gtrless 0 \text{ as } f_i'(k_i) \gtrless \delta .$$

The slope of the free trade $Z_T Z_T$ line is obtained as follows. Substitute (C.13) into (C.12), then substitute (C.1'), (C.5) and use $di = \delta\, dk$ to get

$$(C.20) \qquad di \left[\frac{f_i + \delta(k_c - k_i)}{\delta(k_c - k_i)}\right] = -A \cdot p + \left[\frac{F'(m_c)m_c^2 f_i''(k_c - k_i)}{(F(m_c) - m_c F'(m_c))f_c}\right] dk_i$$

Note that $\dfrac{f_i + \delta(k_c - k_i)}{\delta(k_c - k_i)} = \dfrac{w + \delta k_c + (f_i' - \delta)k_i}{\delta(k_c - k_i)} \gtrless 0$ as $k_c \gtrless k_i$ when $f_i' > \delta$.

This equality can be seen by adding and subtracting $f_i' \cdot k_i$ from the numerator of the left hand side and using equation (3.11). Now using $d(f_i') = f_i''\, dk_i$ we get

(C.21) $$\left.\frac{di}{d(f_i')}\right|_{I_{rT}} = \frac{-\delta\cdot p\cdot A(k_c-k_i)}{f_i''(w+\delta k_c+(f_i'-\delta)k_i)} + \frac{F'(m_c)\delta(m_c(k_v-k_i))^2}{f_c(F-m_cF')(w+\delta k_c+(f_i'-\delta)k_i)}$$

which is equation (3.21) of the text.

The Effects of Changes in Trade Taxes

Totally differentiating the steady state condition for q, which is equation (3.18) gives

(C.22) $$f_i''(k_i)dk_i = 0 \text{ hence } dk_i = 0 \text{ since } f_i''(k_i) < 0.$$

Substituting into (C.1'), (C.2') and C.5) we get:

(C.1") $$dy_c = \frac{f_c}{k_c-k_i}\,dk$$

(C.2") $$dy_i = \frac{-f_i}{k_c-k_i}\,dk$$

(C.5') $$dp = 0.$$

Totally differentiating (3.16') and using (C.5')

(C.23) $$p\,dt = \left[\frac{F(m_c) - F'(m_c)m_c}{m_c^2}\right](dc - dy_c)$$

and substituting (C.23) into (C.12) using equation (C.2") along with $di = \delta\,dk$ to obtain:

(C.24) $$\left[\delta + \frac{f_i}{k_c-k_i}\right]dk = \left[\frac{F'(m_c)m_c^2p}{F(m_c) - m_cF'(m_c)}\right]dt\ .$$

Now note that the expression

$$\delta + \frac{f_i}{k_c-k_i} = \frac{\delta(k_c-k_i) + f_i + f_i'\cdot k_i - f_i'\cdot k_i}{k_c-k_i} = \frac{w + k_c + \delta k_c}{k_c-k_i} \gtrless 0$$

as $k_c \gtrless k_i$ by collecting terms and using (3.18). Hence (C.24) becomes

$$\text{(C.24')} \qquad \frac{dk}{dt} = \frac{F'(m_c)pm_c^2(k_c-k_i)}{(w + k_i + \delta k_c)(F - m_cF')} \gtrless 0 \text{ as } k_c \lesseqgtr k_i$$

which is equation (3.26) of the text.

Substituting (C.1") into (C.23) to get

$$\text{(C.25)} \qquad dc = \frac{p\cdot m_c^2}{F(m_c)-F'(m_c)m_c}dt + \frac{f_c}{k_c-k_i}dk$$

then substituting (C.24') into (C.25) and collecting terms we obtain

$$\text{(C.25')} \qquad \frac{dc}{dt} = \frac{pm_c^2}{F-m_cF'}\left(\frac{w + \delta k_c + \rho k_i + F'(m_c)f_c}{w + \rho k_i + \delta k_c}\right).$$

Since $w = pf_c - pf_c'\cdot k_c = pf_c - f_i'\cdot k_c$ by equations (3.10) to (3.12) and using these equations we get

$$\text{(C.25")} \qquad \frac{dc}{dt} = \frac{pm_c^2}{F-m_cF'}\left(\frac{f_c(p + F'(m_c)) - \rho(k_c-k_i)}{w + \rho k_i + \delta k_c}\right).$$

But $p = F(m_c)/m_c(1+t)$ by equation (3.16') therefore we obtain equation (3.27) of the text as

$$\text{(C.25''')} \qquad \frac{dc}{dt} = \frac{pm_c^2}{F-m_cF'}\ \frac{f_cp(1 - \varepsilon_F(1 + t)) - \rho(k_c-k_i)}{w + \rho k_i + \delta k_c}$$

where $\varepsilon_F = \dfrac{F'(m_c)m_c}{F(m_c)} > 0$ is the elasticity of the foreign offer curve.

SELECTED BIBLIOGRAPHY

Allen, R. D. G. Mathematical Analysis for Economists. London: Macmillan and Co., 1938.

Baldwin, R. E. "The New Welfare Economics and Gains in International Trade." Quarterly Journal of Economics 66 (February 1952):91-101.

Bardhan, P. K. "Optimum Capital Accumulation and International Trade." Review of Economic Studies 32 (July 1965):241-44.

Boyce, W. E., and DiPrima, R. C. Introduction to Differential Equations. New York: Wiley and Sons, 1970.

Burmeister, E., and Dobell, A. Rodney. Mathematical Theories of Economic Growth. New York: Macmillan and Co., 1970.

Burns, M. E. "A Note on the Concept and Measure of Consumer's Surplus." American Economic Review 73 (June 1973):335-44.

Chipman, J.; Hurwicz, L.; Richter, M.; and Sonnenschein, H., eds. Preference, Utility and Demand. New York: Harcourt Brace, 1971.

Diewert, W. E. Harberger's Indicator and Revealed Preference Theory. Technical Report No. 104, The Institute for Mathematical Studies in the Social Sciences. Stanford: Stanford University, 1973.

Divisia, F. Economie Rationnelle. Paris: n.p., 1928.

Foster, E., and Sonnenschein, H. "Price Distortion and Economic Welfare." Econometrica 38 (March 1970):281-97.

Gale, D., and Nikaido, H. "The Jacobian Matrix and Global Univalence of Mappings." Mathematisch Annalen 159 (1965):81-93.

Green, H. A. John. Consumer Theory. Middlesex, Eng.: Penquin, 1971.

Hadley, G., and Kemp, M. C. Variational Methods in Economics. Amsterdam: North Holland, 1971.

Harberger, A. C. "The Incidence of the Corporation Income Tax." Journal of Political Economy 70 (June 1962):215-40.

__________. "Taxation, Resource Allocation and Welfare," in The Role of Direct and Indirect Taxes in the Federal Reserve System. The National Bureau of Economic Research and the Brookings Institute. Princeton: Princeton University Press, 1964.

Harberger, A. C. "Corporation Income Tax," in International Encyclopedia of the Social Sciences. Vol. XV. New York: Crowell Collier, 1968.

_________. "Three Basic Postulates for Applied Welfare Economics: An Interpretive Essay." Journal of Economic Literature 9 (September 1971):785-97.

_________. Taxation and Welfare. Boston: Little, Brown and Co., 1973.

Hicks, J. R. Value and Capital. Oxford: Clarendon Press, 1939.

_________. A Revision of Demand Theory. Oxford: Clarendon Press, 1959.

Hotelling, H. "The General Welfare in Relation to Problems of Railway and Utility Rates." Econometrica 6 (July 1938):242-69.

Inada, K. "On a Two Sector Model of Economic Growth: Comments and a Generalization." Review of Economic Studies 31 (April 1964): 119-27.

_________. "On the Stability of Growth Equilibrium in Two Sector Models." Review of Economic Studies 31 (April 1964):127-42.

Intrilligator, M. D. Mathematical Optimization and Economic Theory. Englewood Cliffs, N.J.: Prentice-Hall, 1971.

Johnson, H. G. International Trade and Economic Growth. Cambridge: Harvard University Press, 1967.

_________. "Trade and Growth: A Geometrical Exposition." Journal of International Economics 1 (February 1971):83-101.

Jones, R. W. "The Structure of Simple General Equilibrium Models." Journal of Political Economy 73 (December 1965):557-72.

_________. "Distortions in Factor Markets and the General Equilibrium Model of Production." Journal of Political Economy 79 (June 1971): 437-59.

Koopmans, T. C. "On the Concept of Optimal Economic Growth," in Semaine d'Etude sur le Rôle de l'Analyse Econométrique dans la Formulation de Plans de Developpement. Vatican City: Pontifical Academy of Science, 1965.

Lerner, A. P. "The Symmetry Between Import and Export Taxes. Economica 3 (August 1936):306-13.

Mieszkowski, P. "On the Theory of Tax Incidence." Journal of Political Economy 75 (June 1967):250-62.

Mohring, H. "Alternative Welfare Gain and Loss Measures." Western Economic Journal 9 (December 1971):349-68.

Oniki, H., and Uzawa, H. "Patterns of Trade and Investment in a Dynamic Model of International Trade." Review of Economic Studies 32 (January 1965):15-37.

Patinkin, D. "Demand Curves and Consumer's Surplus," in Measurement in Economics. Edited by Carl Christ. Stanford: Stanford University Press, 1963.

Rybczynski, T. M. "Factor Endowment and Relative Commodity Prices." Economica 22 (November 1955):336-41.

Ryder, H. E. "Optimal Accumulation and Trade in an Economy of Moderate Size," in Essays on the Theory of Optimal Growth. Edited by K. Shell. Cambridge: M.I.T. Press, 1967.

Samuelson, P. A. Foundations of Economic Analysis. Cambridge: Harvard University Press, 1947; reprint ed., New York: Atheneum, 1965.

________. "The Constancy of the Marginal Utility of Income," in The Collected Scientific Papers of Paul A. Samuelson, Vol. I. Edited by J. Stiglitz. Cambridge: M.I.T. Press, 1966.

________. "Some Implications of 'Linearity,'" in The Collected Scientific Papers of Paul A. Samuelson, Vol. I. Edited by J. Stiglitz. Cambridge: M.I.T. Press, 1966.

Samuelson, P. A., and Swamy, S. "Invariant Index Numbers and Canonical Duality: Survey and Synthesis." American Economic Review 64 (September 1974):566-93.

Schey, H. M. Div, Grad, Curl and All That. New York: W. W. Norton, 1973.

Shell, K., ed. Essays on the Theory of Optimal Economic Growth. Cambridge: M.I.T. Press, 1967.

Silberberg, E. "Duality and the Many Consumers' Surpluses." American Economic Review 62 (December 1972):942-52.

Stiglitz, J., and Uzawa, H., eds. Readings in the Modern Theory of Economic Growth. Cambridge: M.I.T. Press, 1969.

Uzawa, H. "Optimal Growth in a Two Sector Model of Capital Accumulation." Review of Economic Studies 31 (February 1964):7-24.

Williamson, R. E.; Crowell, R. H.; and Trotter, H. F. Calculus of Vector Functions. 2d edition. Englewood Cliffs, N.J.: Prentice-Hall, 1968.

For Product Safety Concerns and Information please contact our EU representative GPSR@taylorandfrancis.com Taylor & Francis Verlag GmbH, Kaufingerstraße 24, 80331 München, Germany

Printed and bound by CPI Group (UK) Ltd, Croydon, CR0 4YY
08/05/2025
01864382-0004